Other Works by Tim Barker

My Jesus Journey
My Jesus Journey: Crescendo
My Jesus Journey: Glissando
My Jesus Journey: Rhapsody
Our Privilege of Joy
God's Revelation and Your Future
Truth, Love & Redemption: The Holy Spirit for Today
The Vision of Nehemiah: God's Plan for Righteous Living
End Times
At Your Feet
Anticipating the Return of Christ
Your Invitation to Christ

The Authentic Christian

Revealing Christ through the Fruit of the Spirit

The Authentic Christian

Revealing Christ through the Fruit of the Spirit

Tim R. Barker, D. Min.

*Superintendent of the South Texas
District of the Assemblies of God*

THE AUTHENTIC CHRISTIAN, Barker, Tim.

1st ed.

Subtitle: Revealing Christ through the Fruit of the Spirit

Unless otherwise noted, Scriptures are taken from the NEW INTERNATIONAL VERSION (NIV): Scripture taken from THE HOLY BIBLE, NEW INTERNATIONAL VERSION ®. Copyright© 1973, 1978, 1984, 2011 by Biblica, Inc.™. Used by permission of Zondervan.

This book and its contents are wholly the creation and intellectual property of Tim Barker.

This book may not be reproduced in whole or in part, by electronic process or any other means, without written permission of the author.

ISBN: 978-1-7358529-6-6

Copyright © 2022 by Tim Barker

All Rights Reserved

Dedication

I dedicate this book study to a treasured group of guys that God brought into my life. What inspires me about this motley crew is their authenticity and vulnerability. They are men just like me who are on a journey to become a better, man, husband, dad, granddad – Christ follower. We meet regularly and/or occasionally to study the Word together and I always leave better than when we started.

Thank you, Brandon, Mark, Eric, Claude, Wayne, Kevin, Kevin, Shavaree, Shane, Doug, Joshua, Larry, Devin & Eric.

Tim R. Barker

Contents

Introduction	i
FRUIT	1
JOY	13
PEACE	27
PATIENCE	38
KINDNESS	50
GOODNESS	63
FAITHFULNESS	77
GENTLENESS	91
SELF-CONTROL	103
About Tim R. Barker	117
A Final Word	119
Study Guide Answers	121
Additional Books by Tim R. Barker	141

Introduction

Appearance. Honesty. Being what we say we are.

This is a challenge even in the world. We must authenticate our credit card via a text, use a password to access our bank account, and carry a photo ID with us when we enter an airport.

We're not who we say we are unless we can prove it.

How does the Christian prove that we are who we say we are? What's our authentication, our password, our photo ID?

That's what this book is about, how we can live a real and honest Christian life that reflects the truth of Jesus living through us.

Matthew 7:15 says to watch out for false prophets. Then, in the next verse, we're told that "by their fruit you will recognize them."

But wait! What fruit? Apples, oranges? No ... so much better.

Follow along as I walk you through the fruit of the Spirit: joy, peace, patience, kindness ... and along the rewarding paths of goodness, faithfulness, gentleness and self-control.

There's a quote by William Shakespeare that says, "If you prick us, do we not bleed?" When the world pricks me, I want to bleed Jesus. I want to be Jesus inside, and when someone cuts me, they get Jesus all over them! Glory! I'm getting excited now!

When you finish this book, you will understand what it means to be an authentic Christian. And I can say from experience, it's the best thing in this world that someone can say about you!

— I —

FRUIT

THE WORLD judges Christianity more by the actions of Christians than it does the preaching of Christians. The authenticity of the Gospel of Christ has more to do with our behavior than all the stories of miracles.

We cannot afford to preach Christ and not be anything like Him!

Would the world accept the following?

A *counselor* – who doesn't get along with other people!

A *teacher* – who doesn't like children!

A *banker* – who doesn't know how to handle money!

An *athlete* – who doesn't like to exercise!

A mountain climber — who doesn't like heights!

The world will not accept a Christian that is not Christ-like, either! We will not win the world for Christ by miracles — we will win the world for Christ when the world sees authentic Christianity lived out in the flesh. The Bible teaches us that God desires godly character above everything else, including ministry!

Matthew 7:15 says to beware:

> *"Watch out for false prophets. They come to you in sheep's clothing, but inwardly they are ferocious wolves."*

Jesus is speaking about the difference of appearance and substance.

False prophets can outwardly look like sheep but inwardly be like wolves! Jesus did not call surface disciples — they had to follow Him through and through!

The Bible teaches that even in the Church there will be sheep and goats together, chaff and wheat … in the end they will be separated. While there are those who can fool others by their appearance, they cannot fool God. The demands of the Gospel do not allow for a sloppy commitment.

Jesus, Paul, and other Apostles warned in their writings about false prophets, false Christs, false followers. Paul even went so far as to say in Romans 16:17: "Now I beseech you, brethren, mark them which cause divisions and offenses contrary to the doctrine which ye have learned; and avoid them." (KJV) It is important to examine our own life and others.

Matthew 7:16-23 gives us a "fruity" lesson:

> *"By their fruit you will recognize them. Do people pick grapes from thornbushes, or figs from thistles? Likewise, every good tree bears good fruit, but a bad tree bears bad fruit. A good tree cannot bear bad fruit, and a bad tree cannot bear good fruit. Every tree that does not bear good fruit is cut down and thrown into the fire. Thus, by their fruit you will recognize them.*
>
> *"Not everyone who says to me, 'Lord, Lord,' will enter the kingdom of heaven, but only the one who does the will of my Father*

who is in heaven. Many will say to me on that day, 'Lord, Lord, did we not prophesy in your name and in your name drive out demons and in your name perform many miracles?' Then I will tell them plainly, 'I never knew you. Away from me, you evildoers!'"

While we are not to judge outsiders or each other's motives, we are to examine the fruit of each other's life! It is not unchristian to examine the fruit of another … in truth, this is all part of accountability as a Christian.

In fact, Jesus said we would know TRUE Christians BY THEIR FRUIT.

Jesus even clarifies that not everyone who does apparently great miracles in His name will necessarily be His servants … fruit is what determines relationship, not ministry. There must be a real quality of fruitfulness in the life of Christ's servants. It's been said that the "Fruit of Spirit" only grows in the "Garden of Obedience." No exceptions to this principle!

Jesus' strong words clearly indicate a deep change in a life, not just the appearance of a change. It is unsettling that Jesus would say, *"Many will say to me* on that day, 'Lord, Lord, did we not prophesy in your name, and in your name drive out demons and perform many miracles?' Then I will tell them plainly, 'I never knew you. Away from me, you evildoers!'" True fruit is the result of a deep connection to Christ, evident in the very character of the life of the one connected.

On one occasion Jesus came to a fig tree which should have had some fruit on it, and when He went to pick a fig and found no fruit whatsoever, He cursed the tree which immediately withered. (Matt. 21:19) Jesus was attempting to make a statement about Israel at the time. Their failure to show any real fruit meant they would now wither. While it was not the season for full fruit, there still should have been a little fruit on the tree at this time or season ... the complete lack of any fruit was unacceptable with Christ.

John 15:1-9 tells the story of Himself as the True Vine:

> "I am the true vine, and my Father is the gardener. He cuts off every branch in me that bears no fruit, while every branch that does bear fruit he prunes so that it will be even more

fruitful. You are already clean because of the word I have spoken to you. Remain in me, as I also remain in you. No branch can bear fruit by itself; it must remain in the vine. Neither can you bear fruit unless you remain in me.

"I am the vine; you are the branches. If you remain in me and I in you, you will bear much fruit; apart from me you can do nothing. If you do not remain in me, you are like a branch that is thrown away and withers; such branches are picked up, thrown into the fire and burned. If you remain in me and my words remain in you, ask whatever you wish, and it will be done for you. This is to my Father's glory, that you bear much fruit, showing yourselves to be my disciples.

"As the Father has loved me, so have I loved you. Now remain in my love."

No one can produce true spiritual fruit without being connected to Christ!

We must be "IN" Christ in order to develop good fruit. Human effort will not do it! It must flow from Christ through us, much as a vine channels its fruit-producing materials through the mother plant before it shows up as fruit on the vine.

Jesus also emphasizes that we must REMAIN in Him to bring fruit to its full development.

It is not enough to have a single experience with Christ; it must be an ongoing relationship. The nature of Jesus' use of the vine/fruit illustration is to demonstrate the absolute nature of producing Christ's nature in our life over time. Healthy fruitfulness happens with a consistent connection.

It could even be said that the kind of fruit our lives produce reveals the source of our commitment. If we are committed to worldly things more than Christ, our life and lifestyle will no doubt reveal this. The kind of character that expresses itself in our daily lives demonstrates to the world the source of our life. Our language, our priorities, our passions, our expenditures, every part of our lives reveals the true nature of what we draw our life from.

Jesus adds an interesting comment about answered prayers, that those who are truly connected to Christ, those whose fruitfulness is the direct result of their being grafted to Christ, can present in prayer their requests and Christ will grant them. Jesus knew that such people will NOT ask selfishly or for personal gain or benefit. If they are truly connected to Christ, their requests will be those things close to the heart of God Himself, so there is little concern about whether it should be answered or not.

When our life flows directly from Christ, our fruit and our passions reflect His heart and life, not our own.

Galatians 5:22 says it like this:

> *"But the fruit of the Spirit is love, joy, peace, forbearance, kindness, goodness, faithfulness ..."*

Once Christ ascended to heaven, He promised His disciples that He would send another just like Him to be with them, in fact, IN them. This was the Spirit of God. With the coming of the Spirit we now have our source of fruitfulness.

The fruit of the Spirit IS LOVE! This in the Greek is singular, not plural (agaph) ... the "FRUIT OF THE SPIRIT IS LOVE ...." The following list of items are not "other" fruits ... they are qualities of LOVE.

The Corinthian Church focused on "charismata" (gifts), but Paul made it clear that "charismata" without character is nothing more than sounding brass and tinkling cymbals. So, in Paul's emphasis in the middle of his discussion on the gifts (chapters 12 and 14) he writes a whole chapter on LOVE ... the fruit of the Spirit (chapter 13). The Corinthian Church was misdirected on spirituality and how they judged it.

ANYONE can be used in the gifts, even baby Christians ... but fruitfulness is the result of maturing processes. The gifts are a function of faith and availability. **The fruit of the Spirit is a function of spiritual development.**

John mentions in his first epistle that no one can say they are connected to God if they fail to LOVE, because LOVE IS the fruit of the Spirit of God. This kind of love is not the natural type, it is the supernatural kind of love. It is love that goes well beyond what is humanly possible.

The world is not as much interested in the claims of Christianity (via the historic issues that might prove it) as they are interested in seeing Christianity that is supernatural in the life of Christ's followers today.

That our lives can matter so much in terms of the authenticity of the Gospel must make us careful to reveal the Christ of the Bible in all our actions and attitudes. What do people see about Christ when they view your life? What fruitfulness do others see when they examine your life? Is the Spirit of God clearly visible in your life?

People tend to associate miracles with spirituality, meaning that if a spiritual leader has lots of miracles in their ministry they are held up in awe. Jesus however taught that a man or woman's character is what shows their level of spirituality.

People are not spiritual because they can do miracles or because they know lots of Scriptures. It is when they express the fruit of the Spirit that they are truly spiritual.

God would rather see fruity Christians vs. nutty ones!

Chapter One
Study Guide

1. Authenticity is the mark of a true Christian. What gives us authenticity in the eyes of the world?

_____

_____

_____

2. Matthew 7:15 speaks of "false prophets." What makes someone a false prophet?

_____

_____

_____

3. In Matthew 7:16-23, we learn how to recognize a true follower of Jesus. Describe the process as illustrated by the Master.

_____

_____

_____

4. What will happen to the Christian who cries, "Lord, Lord," but shows no evidence of good fruit?

_____

_____

_____

5. What is the key ingredient to producing true spiritual fruit in Christ?

_____

_____

_____

6. What is the difference between "gifts" and the "fruit" of the Spirit?

_____

_____

_____

7. Of spiritual gifts and fruit, which is more important and why?

_____

_____

_____

Answers can be found on p 123.

— 2 —

JOY

Biblical "JOY" is one of the most misunderstood attributes of the fruit of the Spirit! Normally when we think of the concept of "JOY" we think in terms of:
- *laughter*
- *smiling faces*
- *no problems, giving elated feelings, carefree rest*
- *bubbling personality*
- *fulfillment without worry*
- *an emotionally high state*
- *without cares*

The truth of the matter however is that "JOY" in the Bible is nearly the opposite of a tranquil situation, and it may or may not have any strong emotions or feelings associated with it.

It is truly amazing how many times phrases like "SING FOR JOY" or "SHOUT FOR JOY" or "SHOUTS OF JOY" and even "LEAP FOR JOY" are used in the Bible (about 73 times in the NIV version of the Bible).

JOY is an essential part of being a Spirit-filled Christian, certainly where the fruit of the Spirit is at work.

The Bible teaches us that JOY is love's strength! It blossoms during tribulation, not after it. It is NOT just an outward expression or feeling, it is an inward confidence in God's love and goodness that gives a strength to our life no matter what we are experiencing.

I Thessalonians 1:6-7 shows us how it works:

> *"You became imitators of us and of the Lord, for you welcomed the message in the midst of severe suffering with the joy given by the Holy Spirit. And so you became a model to all the believers in Macedonia and Achaia."*

Early believers knew tremendous pain and persecution, yet they were the most joyful Christians! It wasn't just suffering that involved a tight budget, it was suffering that meant loss of life and loss of income, even loss of family and friends! Take note that Paul says they welcomed the message of the Gospel "with the joy given by the Holy Spirit" in spite of "severe suffering." (v. 6) How fragile our sense of joy is today ... we can struggle with a heavy schedule or a bad cold, or someone gives us a hard time, and before we know it, we have no joy in the Lord anymore.

Biblical JOY is not an emotion, it is a frame of reference ... a deep work of the Spirit that cannot be shaken by what happens in this world.

Why? Because it is rooted in God, not in the world. In fact, sometimes it is the very process of our struggles and painful events that allow us to experience some of the greatest JOY, especially for those who realize that such struggles can bring out the best qualities of God's graces. For such wonderous saints, such times become the opportunities of JOY.

Many of the disciples and followers of Jesus were said to be full of JOY, yet so many of them perished at the hands of their enemies or faced difficulties beyond our imagination. They discovered a JOY that was deeper than an emotion. They came to experience a state of JOY beyond the concepts of joy the world knows.

2 Corinthians 8:1-3 acknowledges God's opportunities for JOY:

> *"And now, brothers and sisters, we want you to know about the grace that God has given the Macedonian churches. In the midst of a very severe trial, their overflowing joy and their extreme poverty welled up in rich generosity. For I testify that they gave as much as they were able, and even beyond their ability."*

Interestingly, it seems that the greater the degree of difficulty, the greater the degree of JOY!

The Macedonian Churches were undergoing severe financial crisis ... and then Paul has the gall to ask them to contribute finances to help the financially strapped believers in Jerusalem! To the world this would have seemed in poor taste at best, to ask people who were severely hurting to give to others who were also hurting. But Paul understood that the Macedonian Christians would get something back from their giving, GOD'S JOY!

Paul says that even as their poverty was extreme so would be the level of their JOY! Their JOY overflowed! This has always been the way of spiritual realities. There are greater things than just the material things of this world, and even a greater JOY than the happiness the world can offer.

It is no wonder the unbelievers of the first century made statements on how Christians loved one another! The essential quality of a giver is that they are JOYFUL. "...for God loves a cheerful giver!" (2 Cor. 9:7)

JOY'S existence is FOUND in difficulties, not away from them. So often we think we will be joyful when our trials cease, but this is not so.

Some of the most joyful Christians are those who struggle the most while some of the most miserable ones have the least number of struggles.

Hebrews 12:1b-3 says to us:

> *"And let us run with perseverance the race marked out for us, fixing our eyes on Jesus, the pioneer and perfecter of faith. For the joy set before him he endured the cross, scorning its*

shame, and sat down at the right hand of the throne of God. Consider him who endured such opposition from sinners, so that you will not grow weary and lose heart."

Jesus' ability to face the arduous task of the cross came from JOY that He knew WAS COMING IN THE FUTURE. Joy has a power and strength that most do not understand. "Do not grieve, for the joy of the LORD is your strength." (Neh. 8:10)

How do we handle trials that comes our way? We handle them with the same knowledge that no matter what happens to us here in this world there is an eternal reward awaiting us; this JOY gives us strength even when our emotions are struggling.

Our joy is not based in this world, but the world to come. The writer of Hebrews encourages us to "Consider Him who endured … so that you will not grow weary and lose heart." (12:3) Christ's example of JOY giving Him strength for the greatest trial of His life on Earth should be seen as an example for us. Our JOY is found in our relationship to Christ, not in the things of this world.

Take JOY out of the Christian life and you have

a joyless religion! A joyless religion has no power!

John 16:16-22 speaks to our future JOY:

> "Jesus went on to say, 'In a little while you will see me no more, and then after a little while you will see me.' At this, some of his disciples said to one another, 'What does he mean by saying, "In a little while you will see me no more, and then after a little while you will see me," and "Because I am going to the Father"?' They kept asking, 'What does he mean by "a little while"? We don't understand what he is saying.'
>
> "Jesus saw that they wanted to ask him about this, so he said to them, 'Are you asking one another what I meant when I said, "In a little while you will see me no more, and then after a little while you will see me"? Very truly I tell you, you will weep and mourn while the world rejoices. You will grieve, but your grief will turn to joy. A woman giving birth to a child has pain because her time has come; but when her baby is born she forgets the anguish because of her joy that a child is born into the

world. So with you: Now is your time of grief, but I will see you again and you will rejoice, and no one will take away your joy.'"

Jesus' point here is that for the moment, the disciples are going to know mourning ... but that is only for the moment.

This is the point with any trial in a Christian's life: for the moment, trials are painful events, but there is a purpose and a future for those who follow Christ. It is in the same context that Paul could later write Romans 8:28: "And we know that in all things God works for the good of those who love him, who have been called according to his purpose."

At the moment, Jesus says that the world rejoices while we mourn, but a day is coming when this will be reversed. It is hard to be the ones in this world that must endure chiding and persecutions of all sorts, and to stand up to all the mocking of our faith. Too often it seems the world is winning. It seems that those in the world don't pay for their sins or see the consequences of their rebellion against God ... but there is coming a day when we will rejoice and those outside of Christ will wail and gnash their teeth! We must not become shortsighted and lose perspective. This was Jesus' point with His disciples. For Christians, victory is simply an issue of timing! But JOY is our strength during the waiting stages! JOY is a real quality, not just an idea.

Acts 16:22-25 reveals JOY in a PRISON:

> *"The crowd joined in the attack against Paul and Silas, and the magistrates ordered them to be stripped and beaten with rods. After they had been severely flogged, they were thrown into prison, and the jailer was commanded to guard them carefully. When he received these orders, he put them in the inner cell and fastened their feet in the stocks. About midnight Paul and Silas were praying and singing hymns to God, and the other prisoners were listening to them."*

How powerful can this JOY be in our lives? Paul and Silas discovered its strength in the most unlikely place, a jail! After being severely whipped, mocked, and abused they are placed in not just the ordinary prison cell but the inner prison cell ... a really terrible place, and on top of this they are put in stocks and chains! This was harsh treatment and unusually brutal after a severe flogging. Guards sometimes did this to protect themselves from the more dangerous criminals … for if a prisoner escaped, the price tag for the guard was to serve the same punishment of the escaped prisoner. This often meant death for the guard if the prisoner escaped. This explains the guard's action after the earthquake when he thought his prisoners had escaped … he was about to commit suicide rather than go through flogging and then death by the Roman system!

Instead of mourning their situation, instead of wondering where God was when they were severely flogged, instead of crying out over their unfair imprisonment, they begin to sing praises to God in song AT MIDNIGHT!

They are filled with JOY which gives them the strength to worship and praise God in the midst of horrible pain!

Notice that all the other prisoners were listening to them at midnight! It is no wonder that all the other prisoners stayed even after the earthquake loosened everyone's chains … they had to know where these men got the strength to praise God in the midst of pain … even the guard wanted to know!

When others saw Paul and Silas' JOY in the midst of horrible suffering, they wanted to accept this same Jesus that had come into their lives! The guard takes them home and accepts Christ as his Lord! The guard's whole family gets saved also! There is real power in JOY! It gives us the power to persevere under the worst of circumstances!

Christianity would be a whole lot more appealing to others if they saw the JOY that we have in the Spirit and the strength it gives us!

Acts 16:34 reveals the jailer's JOY:

> *"The jailer brought them into his house and set a meal before them; he was filled with joy because he had come to believe in God—he and his whole household."*

Notice that once the jailer had accepted Christ, it states that "he was filled with JOY because he had come to believe in God—he and his whole family." The same JOY that had made it possible for Paul and Silas to praise and worship at midnight while their wounds dripped blood was now in this jailer. Though he had considered suicide earlier and had fallen before Paul and Silas trembling with fear (16:27, 29) he now is unafraid and JOYFUL!

The result of JOY is the proclamation of the Gospel of Jesus Christ! People got saved because of the JOY expressed in the worst of circumstances! What do people see in us when things go terribly wrong? Do they see JOY in us or complaining? What we express in the moments of great trials can have great power in whether others find Christ or not!

JOY is love's strength ... and is found in a Spirit-filled believer! There is incredible JOY possible when we walk in the Spirit. There is incredible strength in God's JOY ... do you have it?

JOY is God's gift of love operating in us even in the midst of suffering and painful events. JOY exists in the presence of pain, not in the absence of it. JOY is love's strength ... because it allows us to endure with confidence in God and keep perspective even in the greatest of trials.

JOY results from the fruit of God's Spirit at work in our lives.

Are you a JOYFUL Christian?

Chapter Two
Study Guide

1. Joy in the Bible rarely indicates a "peaceful" and transcendent state. Yet, joy is intricately intertwined with love. How are joy and love connected?

_____

_____

_____

2. God gives us our greatest opportunity for joy during what times?

_____

_____

_____

3. Paul challenged the Macedonian Churches during one of their most difficult times. What was the challenge and how did it provide an opportunity for joy?

_____

_____

_____

4. Why does Jesus tell us we can be filled with joy even during times of grief?

_____

_____

5. The story of Paul and Silas reveals the secret to turning our joy into our strength during hard times. What lesson can we learn from their time in prison?

_____
_____
_____

6. What is the ultimate result of people seeing the joy of Christ in us?

_____
_____
_____

7. Joy is a fruit of the Spirit. What does it reveal about our relationship with God?

_____
_____
_____

Answers can be found on p 125.

— 3 —

PEACE

The word "PEACE" brings to mind several images. For example:
- *a handshake between two enemies, or a treaty*
- *the laying down of arms*
- *the sunset on a quiet beach*
- *the lack of disturbances*
- *the opportunity of constructive vs. destructive*
- *the freedom from strife and worry*
- *security against all enemies*

PEACE is a goal which mankind has fought wars over! There have been treaties made time and time again to hopefully ensure "PEACE," yet so many times these treaties are violated and short lived.

It seems that everyone wants "PEACE" and yet so

few ever find it. We have weapons of mass destruction in the hopes that their existence alone will keep the peace ... this is peace lived in the shadow of horrible darkness ... a very different kind of "PEACE" than God offers. This world's peace is based on the fear of mutual destruction; God's peace is based on the power of love and His Spirit at work in our hearts. This kind of peace is so different from the world because it is not temporary but permanent; it is internally rather than externally based.

The Bible teaches us that "PEACE" is an inward quality of the fruit of the Spirit, and that even in difficult circumstances it is alive in our hearts as evidence of the work of the Spirit in us.

Romans 5:1-2 says to us:

> *"Therefore, since we have been justified through faith, we have peace with God through our Lord Jesus Christ, through whom we have gained access by faith into this grace in which we now stand. And we boast in the hope of the glory of God."*

When we came to Christ and had our sins forgiven, we experienced something the world has a difficult time comprehending ... "PEACE WITH GOD." Paul states this clearly in this passage. Having been justified by faith, we now have "peace with God." **We are secure in the knowledge that God is now our Lord, He has cleansed us from all our sins, indeed we are in His favor!**

While sin separated us from God, faith in Christ now brings us into fellowship with God. No longer do we exist in guilt! There is a security against guilt that is ours now that we are in Christ. It is not our efforts that bring us this "PEACE," it is the fact that Christ has paid the price and we can now enjoy this freedom from sin, secure in our position before God!

Guilt is one of Satan's weapons against us ... yet God's peace is security against this weapon, for our guilt is gone. Our hearts can be at peace with God because we know that our sins are forgiven. Though Satan is the "accuser of the brethren" (Rev. 12:10) we know that Christ has set us free from guilt and condemnation ... Paul wrote beautifully about this in Romans 8:1: "Therefore, there is now no condemnation for those who are in Christ Jesus." This kind of peace is one that the world does not know nor can it comprehend; it is a peace that goes to the very core of our being!

Colossians 3:15 calls us to peace:

> *"Let the peace of Christ rule in your hearts, since as members of one body you were called to peace. And be thankful."*

Paul tells us that we are to let this "PEACE" RULE in our hearts … we are "called to peace." This means that when we could retaliate, we choose not to, but to let "PEACE" rule instead. This is certainly different from the world's way of getting even when they are wronged! Rather than let our "emotions rule our hearts," we are to let "peace rule in our hearts." This requires a commitment to change the use of our emotions and feelings to do something wholesome instead of something destructive. It is never easy to change the nature of retaliation. We must be willing to completely alter the use of our emotions from destruction to construction. It can be done with God's help and His Spirit at work in our lives. In Christ our lives have a different purpose than the sinful, driven nature we had before.

The same security from guilt that gives us peace that our sins are forgiven gives us the power to forgive others of their sins against us. In this way there is a very powerful security from guilt, both in our relationship with God and with each other! Peace is love's security!

John 14:27 offers us this promise:

> *"Peace I leave with you; my peace I give you. I do not give to you as the world gives. Do not let your hearts be troubled and do not be afraid."*

Jesus clearly tells His disciples that there is a reward for being His followers ... a peace that is way beyond any kind of peace that can be given by man! Mankind's type of peace is very tenuous. We are never quite sure how long it will last or how quickly it will be broken. Because mankind's type of peace can be fleeting, it yields a type of despair and fear ... peace that can disappear so quickly. Christ however states that the peace He gives is very different from this world, for it is neither fragile nor fleeting. It is forever!

When God's peace dwells in our hearts, we can be

at peace even in the midst of terrible circumstances, even incredible circumstances that would normally shake the very foundations of any human hope! Because of this different kind of peace, Jesus says that we never have to be troubled or afraid. **Our security is found in Christ, not this world!**

This reward is not something we have to wait until heaven comes to receive; this is God's gift for those who follow Him NOW! There should be a very real difference between a follower of Christ's attitude about life and the attitude of someone in this world who doesn't know Christ. Jesus' statement, "Do not LET your hearts be troubled and do not be afraid," suggests a certain effort on our part to allow this new attitude to form in us.

Have you discovered the security God has given us through His peace?

Romans 14:17-18 clarifies the purpose of our peace through Christ:

> *"For the kingdom of God is not a matter of eating and drinking, but of righteousness, peace and joy in the Holy Spirit, because anyone who serves Christ in this way is*

pleasing to God and receives human approval."

We must keep in mind however that God's kind of peace is NOT found in the things of this world ... only in Christ!

It is not meat, drink, or any other forms of material things. It is "righteousness, peace and joy in the Holy Spirit." (v. 17) God's peace is rooted in spiritual terms, not physical terms. In this sense God's peace is so much deeper because it goes to the core of our soul rather than the outward appearance of things around us. Worry, fear, and anxiety are epidemic in our culture ... our statistics of those who seek out counseling and drug therapy for anxiety and the rates of depression which are at an all-time high give evidence to the fact that so many do not know God's peace! The problem with the world is that they are seeking deep peace in shallow places ... the things of this world!

God's righteousness however is the basis of our peace ... and the foundation for our security in His love!

We cannot find the kind of peace we all hope for in the things of this world. This is true in the hearts of people today, too. They all want peace but are full of anxiety. Much of what we worry over is outside of our control anyway, but our soul can be controlled by God's Spirit. God is in control, and His Spirit in us gives us internal control so that we can be at peace.

Philippians 4:6-7 tells us how to find peace:

> *"Do not be anxious about anything, but in every situation, by prayer and petition, with thanksgiving, present your requests to God. And the peace of God, which transcends all understanding, will guard your hearts and your minds in Christ Jesus."*

Because our peace comes from eternal things and not temporal things, we do not have to be anxious about anything!

Our security in God's love and work in our lives allows us this freedom from anxiety. Instead of being anxious, we can pray to God whose love always seeks our best. All things being considered, our confidence is no longer in our work, but the will of God ... and so we no longer have to be anxious. The resulting trust in God brings peace. This peace passes all understanding because it is not founded in natural things, it is founded in the supernatural power of God's Spirit at work in our hearts and lives.

God's eternal power changes dramatically our perspective on temporal things; they now seem so small in comparison to God's mighty power. God's peace alters our perception of the much smaller things of this world ... hence why it passes understanding! God's peace guards our hearts and minds in Christ!

God's peace can keep our mind and heart in a state of peace although the things of this world are crazy around us. This kind of peace is real! This kind of peace is powerful! This kind of peace the world can't understand! This kind of peace gives a real security!

Do you know the Peace of God which passes understanding?

Jerusalem means "city of peace" or "possession of peace" — a city whose name almost never rings true! The earthly city doesn't live up to its name. The "new" Jerusalem does however, and as citizens of God's kingdom, we will live in this new Jerusalem. God's Spirit allows His peace to rule in our hearts and minds even now. It is the security of God's love.

How secure are you?

Chapter Three
Study Guide

1. Why is the world's peace always temporary?

_____
_____
_____

2. How is God's peace different from the world's peace?

_____
_____
_____

3. Our peace in God comes through our fellowship with Him. How do we bring this fellowship about?

_____
_____
_____

4. What do our emotions have to do with the peace we wish to find in God?

_____
_____
_____

5. Mankind's peace is very tenuous. Because it can disappear so quickly, how does that affect us as

people?

_____

_____

6. Describe the difference in God's peace that allows the Christian to "not let our hearts be troubled or afraid."

_____

_____

7. The city of Jerusalem has never lived up to its name "city of peace." How/when will that be different in the future?

_____

_____

Answers can be found on p 127.

— 4 —

PATIENCE

The one quality sorely lacking in our culture and society today is "patience!" Just look at our lifestyle. We have instant cereals, instant soup, instant coffee, instant milk, instant credit, instant delivery, instant success books, instant drying glues, instant winners, instant pain relief, instant acid indigestion relief, instant teeth whitening, eyeglasses in less than an hour, instant-on TV sets, even instant hot burners on stoves. Is it any wonder that our Christianity often reflects a similar ring?

We want instant relief from pain and problems — *in other words, "name it and claim it" theology.*

We want instant spiritual maturity — *to teach before we have adequate learning!*

We want instant spiritual authority — *to "bind and loose" and "command & confess" in the name of the Lord without even knowing what that really means.*

We want instant results from ministry — *starting and stopping ministries or moving from place to place if things don't happen fast enough or like we want (often true of both pastors and laypeople).* The truth is that a lack of patience rarely gets us ahead like we think!

The Bible teaches us that patience as an aspect of the fruit of the Spirit in our lives helps to develop stability in our walk with God.

2 Peter 3:4 has this to say:

"They will say, 'Where is this "coming" he promised? Ever since our ancestors died, everything goes on as it has since the beginning of creation.'"

2 Peter 3:9 assures us the Lord is on His way:

"The LORD is not slow in keeping his promise, as some understand slowness. Instead he is patient with you, not wanting anyone to

perish, but everyone to come to repentance."

2 Peter 3:15 makes the connection between patience and salvation:

"Bear in mind that our Lord's patience means salvation, just as our dear brother Paul also wrote you with the wisdom that God gave him."

The world essentially mocks spiritual realities. They scoff at Christians and the Bible for saying that Christ is coming again ... something that we have been saying now for thousands of years! The sinner doesn't see evidence of anything big coming ... everything to them has pretty much stayed the same since the days of creation. This smug attitude is sometimes hard to deal with ... even for Christians!

But, God is not slow concerning His promises ... at least from His vantage point ... but it sure seems that way to us humans!

God's "slowness" is simply His patience at work with sinners ... yes, He may not have yet acted, but this doesn't mean it won't happen, just that it hasn't happened YET! God's patience means salvation for the lost! God is being patient so that many more can have an eternal relationship with Him.

God is patiently enduring both sin and sinners so that some may be saved. God NEVER waits too long on anything.

Remember that next time you think He has messed up or forgotten you. God IS ALWAYS working out some purpose when there are delays … even if those delays are caused by our own mistakes. This is the meaning of Romans 8:28: "And we know that in ALL THINGS God works for the good of those who love Him, who have been called according to His purpose."

Sooner or later the truth of God's reality and the presence of heaven will strike everyone … so much better to be ready now!

Our world judges everything by what it sees NOW, but God's purposes are at work during this time of His patience with sinful man. Sinful man underestimates God and His love … and His plans! (Unfortunately, so do some Christians!) This is not wasted time during His patience; He is creating His people for eternity and His patience now is good news for sinners! Some may not come right away, but perhaps later ... God knows what He is doing!

I Corinthians 13:4 reveals God's patient love:

"Love is patient, love is kind. It does not envy, it does not boast, it is not proud."

Once understood, God's patience results in sinners becoming saints.

The opportunity to turn to God is NOW ... and the change is profound in our lives not only for the present but also for the future! God's patience now becomes our patience! Like God, we are called to have love that shows patience with others ... if God lovingly endured us while we were sinners, we too can learn to be patient with others who are still sinners ... and even those who are saints!

Patience is an aspect of the fruit of the Spirit in our lives. Its presence in our lives allows us to minister gracefully to others even when they don't appear to deserve it.

God's patience with others can also be our patience with others. Patience by its very nature exists only in circumstances where there IS NO ANSWER

NOW. Therefore, to love others with patience probably means that they don't presently deserve it! But, we love patiently in hopes of what will be, even before there is evidence that it will be!

Why does God put up with all the sin and sinners in this world? Why does it seem that the wicked get away with murder while the righteous suffer? Because God is PATIENT – allowing for salvation to occur! Why should we be patient? – for the same reason!

James 5:7-11 is our challenge for patience:

> *"Be patient, then, brothers and sisters, until the Lord's coming. See how the farmer waits for the land to yield its valuable crop, patiently waiting for the autumn and spring rains. You too, be patient and stand firm, because the Lord's coming is near. Don't grumble against one another, brothers and sisters, or you will be judged. The Judge is standing at the door! Brothers and sisters, as an example of patience in the face of suffering, take the prophets who spoke in the name of the Lord. As you know, we count as blessed those who have persevered. You have heard of Job's perseverance and have*

seen what the Lord finally brought about. The Lord is full of compassion and mercy."

In this passage, James calls on all believers to reflect God's attitude of patience, "until the Lord's coming!" **We can't choose to be patient for some things and not others ... patience itself is a virtue God calls us to.**

We usually have no problem being patient with our own spiritual development but a hard time with others around us that seem to be growing slower than we think they should! Spiritual fruit is like natural fruit, it takes time to develop! No farmer plants potatoes today and expects to harvest them that same night! If PATIENCE IS LOVE'S STABILITY, the *lack of patience will be instability!* This is what happens in relationships ... someone loses patience, and all stability is gone. This is what happens in groups, even churches when they lose patience with one another!

The Christian's call is to be patient with ALL ... it not only stabilizes others, but it also stabilizes us!

It is not easy to be patient ... and some have prayed, "Lord, give me patience, and give it to me

NOW!" — sounds like a typical American Christian prayer! God's fruit in our lives demonstrates patience toward ALL, not certain ones. Our lives would be much more stable if we would learn to have patience in what God is doing in us, through us, and in others as well.

When James says not to grumble against one another, he is saying that they had lost their patience with one another — hence the grumbling, "I can't take so-and-so anymore!" James says on the other hand, "As you know, we consider blessed those who have persevered." (9:11a) He is recognizing the stability & happiness ("blessed") of those who have learned perseverance or patience. Tragically we often jump the gun on discontent ... and fail to understand how good we may actually have had it — all because our patience ran out too soon.

We must remember, we are backwards people. Sinners always have their past catching up with them and saints always have their future catching up with them! Since we look forward and not backward, we can be patient because we know what is coming! This gives us stability in the NOW, something people don't have who must worry about their past catching up with them. Granted that things don't always move fast enough for our likes and tastes, but if we are patient, God may surprise us yet! So many Christians have properly missed out on blessings because they acted too soon.

What we need is the wisdom to know when to wait, and when not to!

Many of the best things that come in our life will not come quickly! Success is rarely instant! Healthy finances do not come from instant lottery wins (which ruin a large percentage of people's lives who do win large sums of money instantly!) Character needs time and challenges to develop. Most of what is good in life comes slowly and through boring repetition!

God is patient. He is very stable. In fact, learning to walk in the patience of God encourages our own stability!

DO WE HAVE PATIENCE LIKE GOD? Instead of always reacting impatiently to others, we could act redemptively toward them with patience!

In an age when society demands everything to be "faster" and "now," the attribute of patience can be quite a challenge. While the age of instant coffee and instant credit can meet a quick need, they do not satisfy us long term. Patience gives stability to our lives, and it is a wonderful part of being Spirit filled!

Chapter Four
Study Guide

1. Why does the Word focus so strongly on patience as an aspect of the fruit of the Spirit?

_____
_____
_____

2. We can misunderstand God's patience as being slow concerning His promises. What is God's real reason (from His vantage point) for His enduring patience?

_____
_____
_____

3. We can learn a character lesson from God's patience with us. What does God wish us to learn?

_____
_____
_____

4. Patience is a characteristic of love. How are patience and love connected, and why is patience so important to love?

_____

5. What do we mean when we say that Christians are a backwards people?

6. How do so many Christians miss out on blessings God intends for them?

7. Connect the value of patience with developing our Christian character.

Answers can be found on p 129.

— 5 —

KINDNESS

In a "dog-eat-dog" society, the concept of "kindness" has taken a back seat. New studies have shown that Americans are losing their civility. And of course, it is always someone else who fails to express kindness.

Consider the following percentage of Americans who:

- *think incivility is a serious problem: 89%.*
- *think mean-spirited political campaigns are to blame: 73%*
- *think rock music is to blame: 67%.*
- *think talk radio is to blame: 52%.*
- *think their own behavior is uncivil: 1%.*

Kindness expressed is looked upon suspiciously today ... it is tragic that such an important aspect of

God's power can be viewed by the world as suspicious!

This quality is a must for the Spirit-filled Christian! However, we must not be "kind" to get something back from others, but rather act in kindness because it is God's nature in us to be kind toward others. "... LOVE IS KIND ..." (I Cor. 13:4)

Godly kindness can powerfully transform the world of both sinner and saint ... for the sinner it shows the love and power of God, and for the saint it allows us to experience God's love and power.

2 Corinthians 6:1-13 makes this appeal:

"As God's co-workers we urge you not to receive God's grace in vain. For he says, 'In the time of my favor I heard you, and in the day of salvation I helped you.' I tell you, now is the time of God's favor, now is the day of salvation. We put no stumbling block in anyone's path, so that our ministry will not be discredited. Rather, as servants of God we commend ourselves in every way: in great endurance; in troubles, hardships and distresses; in beatings, imprisonments and riots; in hard work, sleepless nights and hunger; in purity, under-

standing, patience and kindness; in the Holy Spirit and in sincere love; in truthful speech and in the power of God; with weapons of righteousness in the right hand and in the left; through glory and dishonor, bad report and good report; genuine, yet regarded as impostors; known, yet regarded as unknown; dying, and yet we live on; beaten, and yet not killed; sorrowful, yet always rejoicing; poor, yet making many rich; having nothing, and yet possessing everything. We have spoken freely to you, Corinthians, and opened wide our hearts to you. We are not withholding our affection from you, but you are withholding yours from us. As a fair exchange—I speak as to my children—open wide your hearts also."

Paul talks to a group of Christians who were having difficulties being kind to one another. Corinthian Christians were divided into factions in the Church. (I Cor. 1-3) Corinthian Christians were taking each other to court in lawsuits. (I Cor. 6) Corinthian Christians were having marriage difficulties. (I Cor. 7) Unkind things were being said about Paul and his ministry. (I Cor. 8-9) Corinthian Christians were very unkind to one another during communion times. (I Cor. 11) Even their use of the gifts of the Holy Spirit created confusion! (I Cor. 12-14)

In the midst of all this, Paul shares with them the importance of being kind to one another even when embattled with struggles!

At a time when things go wrong, we can easily become BITTER, but Paul calls on them to follow his own example to become BETTER instead ... the vehicle for becoming BETTER during embattled times: KINDNESS! It is interesting how during extremely difficult times some of the best elements of kindness can shine through. In fact, the process of crushing should actually increase our kindness ... if we are full of the Spirit, it will! The very Greek word translated "KINDNESS" (xrestos – "CHRESTOS") is only one letter different from the Greek word for "CHRIST" (Xristos – "CHRISTOS"). The root word of this Greek word was used to reference grapes that had gone through growth, then a crushing process, and then aged so that it became a sweet mellow wine. Kindness too is the result of growth, crushing, and aging, producing a sweet mellow

KINDNESS empowered by the Holy Spirit in us. It is also interesting in that CHRESTOS was a common slave name in Jesus' day, because most people thought the ideal characteristic of a slave or servant was KINDNESS ... Jesus was in a sense CHRESTOS CHRISTOS! (xrestos Xristos) – the kind servant Christ!

Paul's sufferings did NOT make him bitter or jealous of others, even when others abused him ... instead he turned his heart toward kindness driven by the Holy Spirit.

The only way one can express kindness in exchange for sorrow and suffering is if God "enlarges" your heart! This is what Paul says to the Corinthians, he wants them to "open wide their hearts" even as he had opened wide his to them. The same term was used in I Kings 4:29 where it states that God gave to Solomon "largeness of heart" (KJV) so he could rule with kindness. It simply means that the Holy Spirit's presence in our life can make our heart larger than it normally would be ... empowering us to be kind beyond natural kindness.

The world's concept of kindness is merely "politeness" – this is not the same powerful quality of "kindness" which is an aspect of the fruit of the Spirit. It is what made it possible for Joseph to forgive his brothers who had sold him into slavery ... instead when Joseph meets them years later, he treats them "kindly." It made it possible for David to not force the throne away from the fallen King Saul ... instead David is kind to the king even when King Saul sought to kill David! Paul & Silas were kind to the guard who beat them and put them in prison ... and later when the guard and his family were saved, he took the prisoners home and showed them kindness by washing and dressing their wounds.

There is power in kindness!

Paul encourages these Spirit-filled Corinthians to allow the true fruit of the Holy Spirit to flow through them by acts and attitudes of kindness. These Pentecostals that prided themselves on the gifts needed to have a character focus — they needed fruit, not just gifts; character and not just charismata! While the gifts are beneficial to the body, the fruit of the Spirit is beneficial to all! God give us all large hearts!!!!

2 Peter 1:3-10 says to us:

"His divine power has given us everything

we need for a godly life through our knowledge of him who called us by his own glory and goodness. Through these he has given us his very great and precious promises, so that through them you may participate in the divine nature, having escaped the corruption in the world caused by evil desires.

"For this very reason, make every effort to add to your faith goodness; and to goodness, knowledge; and to knowledge, self-control; and to self-control, perseverance; and to perseverance, godliness; and to godliness, mutual affection; and to mutual affection, love. For if you possess these qualities in increasing measure, they will keep you from being ineffective and unproductive in your knowledge of our Lord Jesus Christ. But whoever does not have them is nearsighted and blind, forgetting that they have been cleansed from their past sins. Therefore, my brothers and sisters, make every effort to confirm your calling and election. For if you do these things, you will never stumble."

Kindness does not happen without effort!

Peter says, "MAKE EVERY EFFORT TO ..." It is not an effortless exercise to display true godly kindness! Peter's sense in this passage is that of deliberateness and effort. Kindness does not come naturally to our fallen sinful nature ... but it is to be an expression of our new heavenly nature. Where the Spirit of God dwells there will be kindness! It is part of the fruit of the Holy Spirit. Peter's list of characteristics to add to our character development is very similar to the list in the fruit of the Spirit passage penned by Paul. Here, though, Peter helps us to understand that it is NOT just the Holy Spirit's activity but our effort combined with the Spirit that helps bring about these characteristics — they aren't automatic. God's divine power enables us when we put forth the effort. God's divine power flows through our ACTS of kindness to transform us and others. **Christ performed many acts of kindness which in many cases led to people praising God and becoming followers of Christ.**

There, of course, is always risk involved in kindness ... there were some that rejected Christ even with His acts of kindness ... how many of the 5,000-plus crowd turned away from Christ after He fed them?

The call to be kind however is not dependent on the results we get, it is dependent on the transformed life we have been given in Christ. This is what separates "kindness" from "politeness." Politeness can be phony, for the goal of politeness is to make people feel good. Kindness, on the other hand, can't be faked. Its goal is to reveal God's love to others, and it makes both the other person feel good and the one who is kind!

Peter recognizes that the quality of kindness does grow and develop over time. "For if you possess these qualities in INCREASING MEASURE …"

Christians should become kinder and kinder as the years go by, not more and more bitter! Failure to develop kindness as we grow older means becoming less and less effective in our life and walk with God. You can't miss Peter's words here: "For if you possess these qualities in increasing measure, they will keep you from being ineffective and unproductive in your knowledge of our Lord Jesus Christ." The reason some Christians are never productive with their faith is they have failed to develop kindness in their character! We simply can't show the world a transforming power from God if we have a rough personality and fail to be kind to others!

Kindness is the hallmark of Christian character — it is what lets the world know that there is a different kingdom at work in the world! It sets us apart from the rest of the animal kingdom!

Peter even adds that failure to have "kindness" means a Christian is nearsighted and blind! 2 Peter 1:9 says: "But if anyone does not have them, he is nearsighted and blind, and has forgotten that he has been cleansed from his past sins." Having been cleansed ourselves from our past sins, there is no excuse in failing to be kind to other sinners! It is God's kindness towards us that kept Him from destroying all of us when we were still sinners. We can learn to be kind to others when we take into consideration what God's grace has done for us! Peter's final statement says that those who learn to express these qualities (which includes "kindness") will NEVER FALL! 2 Peter 1:10 continues: "… For if you do these things, you will never fall …" This is a pretty bold statement! When people lose their kindness, they can be in danger of losing their faith and standing before God! Kindness in this sense has a huge personal benefit to it, for it makes us strong not weak — in this sense there is a huge reward even for the one who is kind!

How has God's fruit been developing in your life? Are you kinder today than before? Is your life developing God's kindness more and more as time goes by? Do you treat some people kindly and others poorly? Do you ask God to help you be kind?

Do you make the "effort" to be kind when given a choice?

God's life in us by His Holy Spirit produces the characteristic of kindness as part of the fruit of the Spirit ... be fruitful! In the original language (Greek) the word for "kindness" is "CHRESTOS" – only one letter different from the word for "Christ" ("CHRISTOS"). The root word was used of an old sweet mellow wine – the results of crushing with sweetness added to produce a mellow wine. Kindness is love's conduct – even when we are crushed, God's sweetness in us will produce a mellow spiritual health.

Kindness is part of the fruit of the Spirit – how kind are you?

Chapter Five
Study Guide

1. God's kindness can mean something vastly different for sinners and saints. Describe the difference between the two.

_____

_____

_____

2. Paul lists six ways the saints at Corinth were being unkind to one another. Tell how at least three of these can apply to the modern church.

_____

_____

_____

3. Give three steps to improve kindness in ourselves and in the church body. (Think grapes!)

_____

_____

_____

4. Describe the difference between the world's concept of kindness and that expected of the saints.

_____

_____

5. Kindness is not an automatic fruit of the Spirit, meaning we don't automatically become kind when we receive the infilling of the Holy Spirit. What else does kindness require?

_____

_____

6. The goal of politeness is to make people feel good. Describe the goal of kindness (which can't be faked).

_____

_____

7. What is the personal benefit we derive from showing the kindness of Christ to those around us?

_____

_____

Answers can be found on p 131.

— 6 —

GOODNESS

The idea of being "spirit-filled" is that we are no longer "fleshly-filled!" While our natural character is selfish or self-directed, our new nature in Christ should be other-directed and giving.

Christians MUST be different from the world!

The fruit of the Spirit produces in us the characteristic of "goodness" — but this must not be understood in the sense of natural "goodness" — it is rather supernatural "goodness." People can do "good things" for many reasons other than truly spiritual ones. They may do good things in the hopes that it will buy them favors later. They may do good things to manipulate others or may do good things to enhance their own image. It could be that they may do good things to gain tax credits or other personal benefits.

The "goodness" that is love's character as a quality of the fruit of the Holy Spirit however does not do "good things" for any other reason than that it is now in someone's nature to do good because they are motivated by God's unselfish love rather than self-love.

What the world does not understand is that often some of the people who have done much good in this world are NOT motivated by a desire to get credit as much as they are motivated by God's presence in their life.

The Bible teaches us that God's love produces a "goodness" in our life that is driven by God's Spirit in and through us. This "goodness" is an outflowing of God's love in our life toward others whether they deserve it or not.

Genesis 1:4, 10, 12, 17-18, 21, 25, 31 tells us:

> "God saw that the light was good, and he separated the light from the darkness.
> "God called the dry ground 'land,' and the gathered waters he called 'seas.' And God saw

that it was good.

"The land produced vegetation: plants bearing seed according to their kinds and trees bearing fruit with seed in it according to their kinds. And God saw that it was good.

"God set them in the vault of the sky to give light on the earth, to govern the day and the night, and to separate light from darkness. And God saw that it was good.

"So God created the great creatures of the sea and every living thing with which the water teems and that moves about in it, according to their kinds, and every winged bird according to its kind. And God saw that it was good.

"God made the wild animals according to their kinds, the livestock according to their kinds, and all the creatures that move along the ground according to their kinds. And God saw that it was good.

"God saw all that he had made, and it was very good. And there was evening, and there was morning—the sixth day."

It is interesting that during creation God ended

each day with the same statement, "And God saw that it was good." This was not a brag on His abilities, it was simply a reflection of His character! Creation reflected the very character of God — "IT WAS GOOD." In fact, when He was completely finished, He said, "IT WAS VERY GOOD." (Gen. 1:31)

God's statement thus indicated that creation bore the stamp of His character and He was not simply bragging about His job. This was true with regard to the creation of Adam and Eve also ... they bore the character of God in that they were both GOOD. **God intended for men and women to bear His character of "goodness" — sin took this away, but the infilling of His Spirit restores it in the believer.**

It may appear to the world that there is little difference between their idea of a good man or woman and a good godly man or woman ... the real difference however will be noted at the end of one's life when we stand before God. Unbelievers who think that things are good NOW will discover that their own goodness WILL NOT SUFFICE for entrance into heaven later. We cannot be fooled by the present apparent goodness of the unsaved; it is a false sense of goodness without lasting eternal merits ... no one is saved by their own works.

Proverbs 11:23-25 reveals the difference:

> *"The desire of the righteous ends only in good, but the hope of the wicked only in wrath. One person gives freely, yet gains even more; another withholds unduly, but comes to poverty. A generous person will prosper; whoever refreshes others will be refreshed."*

The writer of Proverbs 11:23-25 indicates a strong connection between "righteousness" and being "good." "The desire of the righteous ends only in good." (11:23a) The writer clearly is showing that the righteous person's desires can only end in good because it is spiritual in nature and not natural! True "goodness" is not natural … the kind of "goodness" that has no thought of self in mind can only be expressed by those who have a spiritual nature as opposed to a fallen nature. The fallen man may APPEAR to be good, but such goodness will have attached to it the goal of gaining something for self out of that goodness.

The NEW NATURE (the redeemed saint) is

good as a simple reflection of God's character, not with intent to gain selfish ends. Acts of goodness by the spiritual man or woman will not take into account personal gain by such acts; they will simply perform acts that are driven by their desire to be God's agents of mercy and grace and to reflect God's very character. Jesus didn't act good to gain anything for Himself. The greatest acts of goodness come from the character of God in us.

This kind of goodness is not driven by self-discipline as much as it is driven by God's character being expressed through us. It is not a work of the flesh but an expression of the Spirit.

Matthew 19:16-22 tell the story of the rich young man:

> *"Just then a man came up to Jesus and asked, 'Teacher, what good thing must I do to get eternal life?' 'Why do you ask me about what is good?' Jesus replied. 'There is only One who is good. If you want to enter life, keep the commandments.' 'Which ones?' he inquired.*
>
> *"Jesus replied, '"You shall not murder, you shall not commit adultery, you shall not steal,*

you shall not give false testimony, honor your father and mother," and "love your neighbor as yourself."' 'All these I have kept,' the young man said. 'What do I still lack?'

"Jesus answered, 'If you want to be perfect, go, sell your possessions and give to the poor, and you will have treasure in heaven. Then come, follow me.' When the young man heard this, he went away sad, because he had great wealth."

A religious well-to-do young man comes to Jesus and asks a very interesting question, "What GOOD THING must I do to get eternal life?"

Like many Jews of his day, there was this idea that one could be righteous by a single good act that would then guarantee salvation. The idea was to do ONE GOOD THING to satisfy God and remove the guilty conscious. "Goodness" cannot be found in a single act; it is found in a relationship with Christ and becomes love's character in us through Christ. Too often fallen man wants some quick superficial way to find salvation, and then they can go back to living as they choose. Though this rich young man lived a pretty good life ... after all he was able to say he kept MOST of the commandments ... he still realized that he was missing some GOOD THING to be saved! It might be interesting to note that Jesus quoted all the commandments concerning man's relationship to man EXCEPT one. Jesus quotes five of the six commandments regarding man's relationship to man (19:18-19) ... but Jesus leaves off one, "Thou shalt not covet." No wonder the man was able to say, "all these I have kept." If Jesus had included the sixth commandment of the second tablet which said, "Thou shalt not covet," this man would not have been able to answer this way ... this was a test by Jesus to see if the man would himself come clean about the commandments. The very fact that the man did not admit the absence of the final commandment shows that he was not really serious about finding the real "GOOD THING" he needed for salvation.

The one "good thing" the man was missing was not a single act, it was the characteristic of "goodness" which would have allowed him to give his wealth to help others ... the response to the sixth commandment of man-to-man relationship: "Thou shalt not covet." While the young man had kept five of these six commandments, there was still the missing one! He even realizes that he is still lacking although he had kept the five commandments Jesus mentioned. Perhaps he was hoping for a single easy act that he could do to satisfy his desire for eternal life ... some superficial way to make the grade!

This is the way of the world, do a few "good" deeds and hope that this will qualify you for heaven someday. Man is so misled as to think that a few good deeds are enough ... so often we miss the bigger picture!

Notice also that Jesus previously asked him, "Why do you ask me about what is good? ... There is only One who is good ..." Jesus is pointing out what I have already said, that "GOODNESS" is God's character, and to ask about doing some "GOOD THING" means having a relationship with God first! He clearly connects the idea of doing a "good thing" with the person of God ... again emphasizing that true goodness springs from the character of God and not from the character of man. In this sense Jesus asks the man to keep the commandments for they represented the heart of one who desired a relationship with God. The rich young man's problem however was that he wanted a single act to guarantee his salvation rather than a true relationship with God, which would have placed expectations on his life such as ministry to the poor. Such a superficial desire to do good will not cut it with God.

God expects something much deeper ... and offers a true "goodness" that will indeed delve much deeper than the goodness of the world!

When Jesus says to him, "If you want to be perfect ..." He does not mean without fault but mature ... the Greek word teleios (teleios) means "mature." What Jesus is saying is simply, "If you really want to show you are mature about all this ...." Like many young men of his day, he wanted to do a single act to show what a "GOOD" guy he was ... but no single act shows someone's character. It is the day-to-day expressions that demonstrate our real maturity and character. Jesus was calling him to surrender his whole life to goodness, not just complete a one-time act ... he had asked what "good thing" he needed to do to inherit eternal life, and Jesus is telling him ... surrender to God so that God's character of goodness will begin to flow out of your life for the rest of your life and not just in a single act. The young man perceived this as a negative expectation however. The Word tells us: "When the young man heard this, he went away sad, because he had great wealth."

It is sometimes hard to surrender to God's ways ... for at the moment they don't always seem that "perfect" ... but in the end they will prove themselves in our lives if we trust Him!

The character of God's "goodness" in us will enable us to trust Him throughout life even when the moment hardly seems fair ... God CANNOT BE ANYTHING BUT GOOD! ... it is His character! And when His Spirit lives in us, it becomes our character, too. This is why the fruit of the Spirit is characterized by "goodness" as one of its qualities. The full fruit of the Spirit will not show through if we don't surrender to the Spirit of God ... and this was the young man's problem. He would not surrender! The question for you and me is: "Have we surrendered?" Are you hoping a single good act here and there will be sufficient for salvation? It will not be! This is why no one is saved by works!

We must embrace God completely to experience love's character of goodness in our lives. How much of God's goodness shines through your life today?

The Spirit-filled Christian's character is goodness! Goodness is the essence of seeking God for others; it is not a focus on self. Goodness is not a single act; it is a development of character to benefit others. Good acts spring from good character in the same way good fruit can only come from good trees. You cannot be spiritual without also being good, nor good without being spiritual.

Chapter Six
Study Guide

1. What is our reason for doing good once we are infilled with the Spirit?

_____
_____

2. During the story of Creation, God repeatedly says, "It is good." Explain why.

_____
_____

3. Why will unbelievers be sorely disappointed even though they think they have lived a "good" life?

_____
_____

4. Why can unbelievers not achieve heaven through their own "goodness" or works?

_____
_____

5. Why was the rich young man so disappointed in

Jesus' answer to the question, "What must I do to have eternal life?"

_____

_____

_____

6. What is vital for us to do before we ask Jesus the question, "What must I do ..."?

_____

_____

_____

7. The essence of goodness involves more than kindness, politeness, or good manners. In fact, it doesn't focus on us at all. What is the true essence of goodness?

_____

_____

_____

Answers can be found on p 133.

— 7 —

FAITHFULNESS

One of the most important qualities in all healthy relationships is "faithfulness." In a culture that emphasizes success, it is difficult for the importance of this quality to be fully appreciated. And yet, when we look at the life and teaching of Jesus, we don't hear ANYTHING about success.

Jesus didn't say, "Well done, you successful servant." He said, "Well done, you FAITHFUL servant."

Even in parables that mention elements of success, the emphasis is on faithfulness and not success — such as the parable of the talents and their investment by all but one wicked servant who never invested the one talent he was given. The focus of the parable was not the doubling of the investments by the others, but their faithfulness to invest. Still, as Christians we live in a culture that values things like success and reputetions ... and faithfulness is hardly ever the focus!

There is a great challenge for Christians living in a culture that has placed other values much higher than faithfulness ... yet it is this very quality that characterizes the fullness of the Spirit in our lives! It is NOT an option in the Christian life, nor is it a value that can be minimized.

The Word of God teaches us that faithfulness IS THE characteristic of a Christian's commitment to Christ.

Faithfulness is love's commitment.

Hosea 4:1-2 says:

> "Hear the word of the Lord, you Israelites, because the Lord has a charge to bring against you who live in the land: "There is no faithfulness, no love, no acknowledgment of God in the land. There is only cursing, lying and murder, stealing and adultery; they break all bounds, and bloodshed follows bloodshed."

Hosea found himself in a culture similar to ours today. Israel was coming to the end of a very prosperous time in her history. Corruption within institutions, religion, and politics was extremely high. There was plenty of religion but little true worship of God. Religious leaders compromised their own morality to gain financial benefits and political power. Sexual immorality was rampant within the society of Israel, encouraged by the sensual nature of the Baal worship. There was wide toleration of a variety of vices, and those who spoke out against such lax morality were ridiculed and mocked. The institution of marriage was in serious trouble throughout Israel, evidenced even within Hosea's own marriage. (Some things never change!) Faithfulness was not exactly considered an important quality; success, power, influence, tolerance, freedom … these were the emphasized qualities within the culture. Hosea's call to commitment and faithfulness was largely ignored.

He even named his children with the hopes that Israel would get the message from his own children's names! Their names "Jezreel" meant "dispersion" and "Lo-rohamah" meant "not beloved" … yet they still didn't respond! Those who did practice a life of faithfulness were probably considered "old fashioned" and basically unimportant, naïve and uninformed.

The focus and calling of Hosea for his life was to demonstrate FAITHFULNESS as well as call for it. He married an adulterous woman and remained faithful to her despite her constant drifting into an immoral lifestyle. He called on his wife to change her ways and loved her faithfully to draw her towards this. In this way he mirrored God's faithful love for His wayward people, and His call for them to REMEMBER, REPENT, and RETURN to Him. God's people needed a radical FAITHFULNESS, a return to a commitment NO MATTER WHAT!

This is the kind of commitment Christ calls us to. There is no room for a "casual" relationship with God!

How strong is your commitment to being faithful to God? Is it based on how good you feel? Is it based on how well things are going? Is it based on what you want? Or is it based on an absolute commitment to Christ NO MATTER WHAT? Faithfulness can be a huge challenge in an ungodly culture, but it must not be compromised!

Hosea 4:3-4 reveals a harsh rebuke:

> "Because of this the land dries up, and all who live in it waste away; the beasts of the field, the birds in the sky and the fish in the sea are swept away. But let no one bring a charge, let no one accuse another, for your people are like those who bring charges against a priest."

The moral underpinnings of Israel's existence as a once godly nation were gone! There were still some within the nation that held true to God, but they were no longer a nation that worshiped God. The unraveling of their moral underpinnings led to the collapse of their institutions and relationships. In the process they had become preoccupied with success rather than faithfulness.

And yet, this is precisely where America is today! There are some voices still speaking for character and faithfulness, but how many are listening?

Hosea declares an interesting dynamic in his statements here about Israel's moral collapse ... the environment was becoming damaged and was suffering due to the lack of responsible living by faithful citizens. Not even their wealth or government programs were working to preserve the environment! (4:3) The point is simple: As goes the spiritual, so goes the material realm! We would do well to heed this in our country. Also note that when we are faithful to God, we are faithful to His creation ... faithfulness is a quality that works its way through every system of life. Why would this be so? If people only care about what they get, they are not likely to care about what they give ... and faithfulness is all about giving!

Faithfulness is required NO MATTER the results ... and while "success" may not always result from faithfulness, it is still faithfulness that God values and rewards even when success eludes us!

This again can be a difficult concept for Christians in a culture (or a church) that can't get faithfulness out of its citizens unless there are some "guarantees" involved like success, wealth, power, etc. God's character is faithful no matter what. And if His Spirit lives in us, the same characteristics should show in our life!

Hosea 4:6-12 describes a faithless people:

"My people are destroyed from lack of

knowledge. Because you have rejected knowledge, I also reject you as my priests; because you have ignored the law of your God, I also will ignore your children. The more priests there were, the more they sinned against me; they exchanged their glorious God for something disgraceful. They feed on the sins of my people and relish their wickedness. And it will be: Like people, like priests. I will punish both of them for their ways and repay them for their deeds. They will eat but not have enough; they will engage in prostitution but not flourish, because they have deserted the Lord to give themselves to prostitution; old wine and new wine take away their understanding. My people consult a wooden idol, and a diviner's rod speaks to them. A spirit of prostitution leads them astray; they are unfaithful to their God."

Israel's passion for prosperity and success rather than a passion for qualities like faithfulness had actually produced a callousness toward spiritual things. God's Word had been rejected. Even the religious leaders ignored God's Word. They probably thought it too crazy to really believe that written Scriptures could actually be God's Word! Though the priests didn't teach God's Word anymore, they did try to keep the people coming to services since their portion of payments were their cut of the best meat of the sacrifices. They evidently found ways to keep the people bringing sacrifices so they could feast and get rich off the people they ministered to! The priest's own lives however were no better than the compromising culture they lived in, and the results were disastrous spiritually for everyone! They may have continued teaching moral lessons, but they figured no one would listen so they themselves didn't listen to their own teaching! They said one thing out of one side of their mouths and practiced another thing at the same time!

Tragically, the more Israel compromised, the more they wandered away from God; and the more they attempted to move toward success and prosperity, the emptier their lives became!

This is the case today, too ... success has not made Americans happier or more satisfied, in fact just the opposite. Rather than gaining, we are losing when we move away from faithfulness to God. Israel never did listen to Hosea or turn ... and shortly after Hosea's day, the Northern Kingdom called Israel was destroyed ... and never did recover! May God help us before we move down that same path fully! And, while it is always easier to cry out against our nation and her sins, what about OUR FAITHFULNESS? Where are we headed?

Galatians 5:22, 24-25 outlines our redemption:

"But the fruit of the Spirit is love, joy, peace, forbearance, kindness, goodness, faithfulness ... Those who belong to Christ Jesus have crucified the flesh with its passions and desires. Since we live by the Spirit, let us keep in step with the Spirit."

The very characteristic of the Spirit-filled life is FAITHFULNESS! Such fruit is the result of being Spirit-filled.

Faithfulness IS commitment ... first to God and then to others. The fruit of the Spirit is the very character of the Spirit of God, and He can be nothing LESS THAN FAITHFUL! There is no sense of doubt in the statement by Paul, "The fruit of the

Spirit IS ... FAITHFULNESS" – there is no room for flexibility as to whether there IS or ISN'T by the statement. **Christians cannot "choose" whether they will be faithful or not; this is not like buying a car where we have "options" ... it is STANDARD EQUIPMENT for the Spirit-filled believer.** There are institutions in this world where the concept of faithfulness is so absolute that it is not negotiable, and if the world can even recognize under certain circumstances how absolute the quality of faithfulness must be, why can't we in God's Church!?

The United States Army understands that in warfare ABSOLUTE FAITHFULNESS is a must! They also understand that even BEFORE entering the war this must be practiced and learned so that it is second nature when you face the enemy, or too many innocent lives will be lost.

What about our faithfulness to God? What about our faithfulness to His church? What about our faithfulness to our brother and sister in Christ? What about our faithfulness to the lost of this world? ARE WE ABSOLUTELY FAITHFUL, or does it only show when our lives are successful by the standards of this world or our own?

It is quite clear that while this quality of faithfulness flows out of the fruit of the Spirit in our lives, it is also the responsibility of us to act out a commitment for it to be realized.

On the heels of Paul describing the fruit of the Holy Spirit, he says, "And they that are Christ's have crucified the flesh ..." This requires a commitment on our part as well as the work of the Spirit on God's part. Jesus certainly demonstrated this very same cooperation between "spirit" and "flesh" ... He WILLED himself to do HIS FATHER'S WILL ... while empowered by the Holy Spirit ... our model to follow! Faithfulness does not just come from "autopilot" by God's Spirit, it is also our commitment which must be unwavering, too. It is the balance Paul states in verse 25, "If we live by the Spirit, let us also walk in the Spirit." The signature of our life needs to be FAITHFULNESS! Is it yours? If the Marines can hold high their signature as "SEMPER FI" ("always faithful") certainly God's army must also!

Faithfulness is the basis of all healthy things — whether the laws of physics being faithfully the same through time so the universe is predictable and all things hold together, or our relationship to God and others remaining faithful so they remain constant and strong. Remove faithfulness from any system of relationships and deterioration occurs.

Love's commitment is faithfulness — is this aspect of God's Spirit showing in your life?

Chapter Seven
Study Guide

1. Our modern culture values success over many other things, yet Jesus never taught on success. What did the Master prioritize instead and how do we know?

_____

_____

_____

2. Hosea saw the faithlessness rampant in Israel. How did the prophet attempt to redirect the nation back onto the righteous path that God required?

_____

_____

_____

3. What result did Israel's faithlessness have besides the moral and spiritual degradation of the nation?

_____

_____

_____

4. As Israel continued to chase success and prosperity rather than faithfulness to God, what happened in their lives?

_____

5. What happens to a people when God's call to return to faithfulness is ignored on an ongoing basis?

6. How important is it to "choose" faithfulness when we are infilled with the Holy Spirit?

7. Our faithfulness to God can be related to the U.S. Marine's signature motto. What is it and what does it mean?

Answers can be found on p 135.

— 8 —

GENTLENESS

In a culture of rough-and-rugged individualism, gentleness is thought of as weakness, being soft and virtually spineless. Not so! Biblical gentleness is strength under control. In fact, the Greek word translated in Galatians 5:23, "Gentleness," came from a term that was used of a wild horse that had become obedient to the bit and bridle. It was therefore not the lack of power, but great power under the control of a master. Christianity is NOT for the weak! Being a Christian does NOT mean being soft-spoken, weak, or easily intimidated. Rather, it is strength under the control of a master! Gentleness means finding a loving and kind way to do a tough job. It means a control over one's own life and situations in a way that allows kindness and compassion to show through. Gentleness is not being afraid to do what is needed.

The Bible teaches us that GENTLENESS is LOVE'S HUMILITY, strength under control ... this differs from the last element of the fruit of the Spirit, "self-control," in the sense that this quality is "God-controlled" rather than "self-controlled."

Matthew 11:29-30 gives us the Master's words:

> *"Take my yoke upon you and learn from me, for I am gentle and humble in heart, and you will find rest for your souls. For my yoke is easy and my burden is light."*

Jesus tells us to take His YOKE upon us, to learn from Him because He IS GENTLE and HUMBLE in heart ... and if we do, we will find REST for our souls!

"Take my yoke upon you and learn from me, for I am gentle and humble in heart, and you will find rest for your souls." What does this mean? It simply means to stop running on your own strength (expressed through your fallen nature) and submit to the control of God in your life. These yokes were double yokes, and most Jews would "break in" a new ox by yoking them to a seasoned and fully developed ox. The seasoned ox would control by its shear strength the undisciplined ox. The new ox had no choice but to follow the mature ox around. The mature one led the way, did most of the work, and responded completely to the master. The new ox's workload was actually quite easy since the big ox was the one doing most of the work ... but it was training the new one in spite of all the resistance it gave at first. Once yoked, the new ox had little choice if it wanted a life of peace ... if it constantly bucked, it ended up sore and bruised and exhausted, for it was no match for the seasoned strong ox.

How many Christians find their lives miserable? If they do, it is because they are bucking against God's leading in their life and they are fighting against God's strength ... you can't win doing this!

Rest came from working WITH the seasoned ox ... and it also meant a light burden since the seasoned ox did most of the work. The seasoned ox did not kick or bite the new ox, it just kept going in the right direction. The seasoned ox has no need to draw attention to himself; he just HUMBLY does his work.

One of the clear qualities of a Spirit-filled gentle Christian is humility!

When Jesus says, "For my yoke is easy and my burden is light," He is not saying it is easy being a Christian but that it is easy on us when we don't fight Him as a Christian! His burden is light and the yoke is easy when we submit to His control in our lives. When we fight, it is just the opposite! In fact, fighting God only makes us weaker because it will drain our strength, but submitting means developing strength by following Him. The obedient person is not perfect, just smart!

Obeying Christ appears to the world as a weak way to live, and yet it is just the opposite! Living for Christ by obeying His commands makes people of the world uncomfortable because it means yielding up control of one's life. Our culture sees this as a weakness, but it is precisely this yielding that allows us to do things the world cannot do! Such as keeping our passions under control. Such as forgiving others!

The natural man does not forgive easily! The spiritual person DOES forgive, for he or she is enabled to forgive others because they themselves have been forgiven! Our burden is light because Christ has showed us the way and given us the strength to make the journey. **He is conditioning us by His Holy Spirit to be like Him!**

Numbers 12:1-10a tells this story:

> *"Miriam and Aaron began to talk against Moses because of his Cushite wife, for he had married a Cushite. 'Has the Lord spoken only through Moses?' they asked. 'Hasn't he also spoken through us?' And the Lord heard this. (Now Moses was a very humble man, more humble than anyone else on the face of the earth.) At once the Lord said to Moses, Aaron and Miriam, 'Come out to the tent of meeting, all three of you.' So the three of them went out. Then the Lord came down in a pillar of cloud; he stood at the entrance to the tent and summoned Aaron and Miriam. When the two of them stepped forward, he said, 'Listen to my words: When there is a prophet among you, I, the Lord, reveal myself to them in visions, I speak to them in dreams. But this is not true of my servant Moses; he is faithful in all my*

house. With him I speak face to face, clearly and not in riddles; he sees the form of the Lord. Why then were you not afraid to speak against my servant Moses?' The anger of the Lord burned against them, and he left them. When the cloud lifted from above the tent, Miriam's skin was leprous—"

Moses found himself in a difficult situation ... his own brother and sister had turned on him! How often do Christians find themselves in situations where their own brothers and sisters in Christ become jealous and turn on them? No doubt it was a case of jealousy! They used his marriage to a non-Jew as the point of their attack ... often jealous people will use things against us that are really NOT the issue! They felt they were used by God too in great ways ... so why was Moses top dog? It is interesting to note that GOD heard their gripes ... God hears our gripes about others, and HE isn't pleased! "'Has the LORD spoken only through Moses?' they asked. 'Hasn't he also spoken through us?' And the LORD heard this." Miriam and Aaron were out of control! God however sees Moses as one who is under control ... God says

Moses is "very humble, more humble than anyone else on the face of the Earth." The concept here in Hebrew is the same as "Gentleness" in Galatians 5:23. Moses demonstrates his humility in the face of jealous accusations by saying nothing!

A humble believer doesn't feel the need to rail against his critics. He is under control ... it is the natural man that speaks great boasts!

God stepped in to defend Moses. Moses felt no need to do so himself. All three are summoned by God to appear at the entrance to the Tent of Meeting ... right before God's presence! God called Aaron and Miriam to step forward without Moses. God shares with them how He is willing to use them as prophetess and priest by speaking to them via visions and dreams, but with Moses He talks face to face as one friend to another! Their out-of-control attitude toward another servant of God's will now cost them humiliation and pain, for pride comes before a fall! Moses shines as an example of one who even though offended has a different way of dealing with it.

The natural man would strike back, but the spiritual man is under control and gets things done with a gentleness that is only God-breathed!

Numbers 12:10-16 is Moses' cry for mercy:

> *"'Do not let her be like a stillborn infant coming from its mother's womb with its flesh half eaten away.' So Moses cried out to the Lord, 'Please, God, heal her!' The Lord replied to Moses, 'If her father had spit in her face, would she not have been in disgrace for seven days? Confine her outside the camp for seven days; after that she can be brought back.' So Miriam was confined outside the camp for seven days, and the people did not move on till she was brought back. After that, the people left Hazeroth and encamped in the Desert of Paran."*

If Moses had responded in the natural, he might have yelled, "HA, serves you both right, see if you give me a hard time again!" Aaron immediately responds by crying out to Moses for compassion! No doubt Miriam must have looked toward her brother, Moses, too, for help! Moses immediately cries out to God to heal his sister! What an act of "Gentleness!" Rather than take delight in their suffering, Moses cries out for them to be restored. Moses is not thinking of himself, only the wellbeing of Aaron and Miriam and their ministry within Israel. This is the quality of "gentleness" at work, the obvious work of the Holy Spirit in the life of Moses. No doubt this act of love and compassion on Moses' part had a great impact on his relationship with Miriam and Aaron following this.

An act of love and kindness can dramatically change even the hardest soul!

Miriam is required to stay "unclean" the prescribed seven days outside the camp according to Leviticus 14:9 before she is allowed to return. Moses' love for her and her healing as well as Israel's love by stopping and waiting for her full return was an act of gentleness consistent with the quality of the fruit of the Holy Spirit. Gentleness and graciousness are the expression of a strong individual, one controlled by God rather than their own passions and desires. Moses' ability to forgive and even restore his jealous sister is testimony to what God had said about him, that he was indeed the meekest ("gentle" or "humble") man in all the Earth.

No wonder Jesus said in the Beatitudes, in

Matthew 5:5, "Blessed are the meek, for they will inherit the earth." Meekness or gentleness is a quality that cannot be absent from a Spirit-filled Christian. It is what allows us to conquer the world ... for it is strength under control – God's control! The next quality, "self-control," is what allows us to conquer ourselves, but this quality of "gentleness" lets us conquer the world! Are you truly a "gentleman" (or a "gentlewoman")? The term "gentleman" no doubt came from the idea of a strong, controlled male who is humble and gentle, a biblical foundation for such a term.

God, give us Christians whose lives demonstrate the quality of gentleness! Be filled with the Spirit!

"Gentleness" in our culture suggests "soft, easy-going, almost weak!" This quality however is anything but weak! The Greek word translated "Meek" or "Gentleness" is found also in the Beatitudes, "Blessed are the meek," and Jesus said that such "meek" people will "inherit the Earth" ... and in the passage of the fruit of the Spirit the same word is used and translated "gentleness." It literally meant a wild horse that had become obedient to the bit and bridle.

In other words, strength under control!

Chapter Eight
Study Guide

1. Gentleness in the Bible means something other than soft-spoken or easily intimidated. Where did this term for "strength under control" originate?

_____
_____
_____

2. What aspect of "LOVE" does "GENTLENESS" reveal?

_____
_____
_____

3. Jesus asks us to "take His yoke upon us." Describe an easy way to picture what He means.

_____
_____
_____

4. What is the companion aspect of the attribute of gentleness? (Hint, think of Moses.)

_____
_____
_____

5. Why does living for Christ make so many people in the world uncomfortable?

_____

_____

_____

6. Does being used by God give us the right to speak ill of those we disapprove of? Explain your answer.

_____

_____

_____

7. Give another word for gentleness and where we find it in the Bible.

_____

_____

_____

Answers can be found on p 137.

/ — 9 —

SELF-CONTROL

One of the greatest dangers in life is not from an outside source! **The greatest danger a person can face is an undisciplined life!**

There have been those who nearly conquered the world but never themselves, men like Napoleon, many of the Herods, Alexander the Great, and even many of the Pharaohs of Egypt. We have seen this failure even in our modern political leaders whose discipline over their own lives was sorely lacking though they led this great nation. Success in conquering others but failing to conquer self makes men and women unproductive, unfulfilled, sometimes broken and depressed ... which many of these leaders experienced.

Much of the unproductiveness, pain, and

unhappiness in our culture today is the result of undisciplined lives. Greatness does not come from power over others, it comes from power over self. It is a terrible lie that it does not matter how a leader lives his/her own personal life as long as he governs well — the example of an undisciplined life will only encourage another generation of undisciplined lives!

Victory and happiness do not come from what we have but who we are.

Love can become lust without self-control.
Faith without self-control becomes fanaticism.
Pride without self-control becomes arrogance.
Courage without self-control becomes craziness.
Joy without self-control becomes giddiness.

It is impossible to be what God wants us to be without self-control.

The Bible teaches us that an undisciplined life results in terrible losses. No one is truly victorious in life without real self-control.

Romans 8:20-25 provides insight:

> *"For the creation was subjected to frustration, not by its own choice, but by the will of the one who subjected it, in hope that the*

creation itself will be liberated from its bondage to decay and brought into the freedom and glory of the children of God. We know that the whole creation has been groaning as in the pains of childbirth right up to the present time. Not only so, but we ourselves, who have the firstfruits of the Spirit, groan inwardly as we wait eagerly for our adoption to sonship, the redemption of our bodies. For in this hope we were saved. But hope that is seen is no hope at all. Who hopes for what they already have? But if we hope for what we do not yet have, we wait for it patiently."

2 Timothy 3:1-4 paints the darker side of this coin:

"But mark this: There will be terrible times in the last days. People will be lovers of themselves, lovers of money, boastful, proud, abusive, disobedient to their parents, ungrateful, unholy, without love, unforgiving, slanderous, without self-control, brutal, not lovers of the good, treacherous, rash, conceited, lovers of *pleasure rather than lovers of God—"*

In a single moment of failed self-control, the Universe was plunged into sin! This distortion of God's design for humans has left the entire human race prone to being out of control. Paul describes life in the Universe now as "Groaning." (8:22-26) Tragic as the first moments of failed self-control were, each additional moment where self-control was absent only plunged mankind into ever-deepening rifts of tragedy.

This horrible condition hit a real low in Noah's day when every man did evil in the sight of the Lord … where all self-control was abandoned! It again hit a low point during the time of the Judges when the Bible states in Judges 17:6: "In those days Israel had no king; everyone did as he saw fit."

Paul says in 2 Timothy 3:1-4 that the last days will be characterized by the lack of self-control: "But mark this: There will be terrible times in the last days. People will be lovers of themselves, lovers of money, boastful, proud, abusive, disobedient to their parents, ungrateful, unholy, without love, unforgiving, slanderous, without self-control, brutal, not lovers of the good, treacherous, rash, conceited, lovers of pleasure rather than lovers of God—"

Each time history has seen an explosion of undisciplined lives, the stage has been set for judgment. Even the world at times has recognized the absolute importance of self-control for success in life. Our armed forces could not exist nor could our military strength without major amounts of self-control! It is not likely that you will live a successful Christian life without well-developed self-control. Sin is a reality, and victory as a Christian will hinge on the right kind of self-control. The predicament we are in is simple.

We are sinners, and even when saved by grace, our lives cannot continue to be a success without self-control.

Thankfully we are not alone in our self-control! God has made a special provision available in order to be self-controlled. The Holy Spirit has been given to all believers for the sake of helping us in our weaknesses. BUT, while the Holy Spirit helps us, we must also exercise self-control! God does not remove our free will in the exercise of our lives even after we are saved. In fact, we aren't really free until we are saved ... we are now free to be self-controlled. God's Spirit is thus teaching us, training us ... but we must yield to that training and exercise our self-control made possible now by God's power in our lives. The world may not understand this process, but we must not ignore it!

The world can't understand how a Holy Spirit can possibly make things different ... but they will understand the results if they see us yielded to God and our lives self-controlled.

Does your life reflect the training of the Holy Spirit or the values of this world? The world will judge us more by what they see in our lives than what they hear us say.

A self-controlled godly life will teach more about the nature of God than all the theology books in a library!

I Corinthians 9:24-27 gives this example:

> *"Do you not know that in a race all the runners run, but only one gets the prize? Run in such a way as to get the prize. Everyone who competes in the games goes into strict training. They do it to get a crown that will not last, but we do it to get a crown that will last forever.*

Therefore I do not run like someone running aimlessly; I do not fight like a boxer beating the air. No, I strike a blow to my body and make it my slave so that after I have preached to others, I myself will not be disqualified for the prize."

Paul mentions the fact that in a race all the runners run, but only the MOST disciplined person usually wins … so we are to run FOR THE PRIZE.

The self-control we exercise in this life does have a focus, both now and in eternity. The Olympics will start one day. Imagine how many undisciplined athletes will be there … NONE! The level of self-control can actually determine the quality of our life as well as the rewards of our life … both now and in eternity! Athletes don't accept excuses. Only those who lack self-control have a myriad number of excuses. Judges don't accept excuses either! Imagine telling a judge at the Olympics that you were just too busy to train since the last Olympics four years ago, so you hope that the judge will be easy on you. If you want the prize, you must accept the self-control that comes with getting it! We cannot choose to become a believer and then expect to ignore God's call for self-control in our lives.

For those who learn to have self-control, the rewards can be sweet. We must not forget what is most important.

Self-control is required for every step of our lives. There will never come a time where we can avoid it. God has marked out the course, and we must accept the course and follow His plan if we would enjoy the rewards He also has for us. We can spend a lot of wasted time either manufacturing excuses for our lack of self-control or trying to explain our reasons for ignoring self-control … but it will not change anything for the better. Paul even states how important it was for him as a leader to be sure that his own life reflected strong self-control while he preached it to others or he himself could lose the prize.

Real leaders have a great deal of self-control in their lives. Such self-control should be evident to all.

I Corinthians 10:1-13 tells us:

> *"For I do not want you to be ignorant of the fact, brothers and sisters, that our ancestors were all under the cloud and that they all*

passed through the sea. They were all baptized into Moses in the cloud and in the sea. They all ate the same spiritual food and drank the same spiritual drink; for they drank from the spiritual rock that accompanied them, and that rock was Christ. Nevertheless, God was not pleased with most of them; their bodies were scattered in the wilderness.

"Now these things occurred as examples to keep us from setting our hearts on evil things as they did. Do not be idolaters, as some of them were; as it is written: 'The people sat down to eat and drink and got up to indulge in revelry.' We should not commit sexual immorality, as some of them did—and in one day twenty-three thousand of them died. We should not test Christ, as some of them did— and were killed by snakes. And do not grumble, as some of them did—and were killed by the destroying angel.

"These things happened to them as examples and were written down as warnings for us, on whom the culmination of the ages has come. So, if you think you are standing firm,

be careful that you don't fall! No temptation has overtaken you except what is common to mankind. And God is faithful; he will not let you be tempted beyond what you can bear. But when you are tempted, he will also provide a way out so that you can endure it."

Israel serves as a great example of the possibilities of self-control, and the results when such control is absent. All the Israelites had experienced equal realities, both with God and each other ... and so many of them perished through failed self-control. They now serve as a warning to us to not follow such an undisciplined life. Less than a handful of Israelites who left Egypt made the Promised Land. It was the constant lack of self-control by the vast majority that took them from one disaster to another, and it was the basis of their constant grumbling! Generally speaking, people who complain a lot are usually undisciplined people ... their complaints help them excuse their own lack of self-control by putting the blame on others. It has always been true that both possibilities exist for our lives, darkness and deliverance ... and so much of this comes from either the lack of self-control or the exercise of it.

How productive is your life? How fruitful has your life been? Is your life a demonstration of self-control that others can admire and follow?

It takes a narrow focus to be self-controlled ... but this will keep us moving in the right direction.

All of us face the same temptations (10:13), we have the same opportunities (10:1-4), AND the same need for self-control if we are to be a success spiritually and otherwise.

Self-control is love's victory. Are you living victoriously?

Of the eight characteristics of the fruit of the Holy Spirit, seven are directed either Godward or manward ... this last one however is directed selfward! No progress in a believer's life can occur without this final quality, for "SELF-CONTROL is LOVE'S VICTORY!" The undisciplined life will be a disaster spiritually and otherwise.

How victorious is your life?

Chapter Nine
Study Guide

1. Why is it so important to learn self-control in our Christian walk?

_____

_____

_____

2. Self-control not only affects us, but it also affects others, too. Who is most affected if we fail to exhibit self-control?

_____

_____

_____

3. The Universe seems peaceful and orderly, with planets and even galaxies right where we expect them to be. How do we know this "peacefulness" is not the case?

_____

_____

_____

4. Salvation is given to us without cost, and we are saved by grace. Yet, to maintain a committed life in Christ, what else is necessary?

5. Paul compares salvation to a race. What must all contestants do to come in first place?

6. How did Paul see himself differently as a leader in the early Church?

7. Of the eight characteristics of the fruit of the Spirit, only one (self-control) is directed back at us. Why is this concept so vital in our Christian walk?

Answers can be found on p 139.

About Tim R. Barker

Reverend Tim R. Barker is the Superintendent of the South Texas District of the Assemblies of God which is headquartered in Houston, Texas

He is a graduate of Southwestern Assemblies of God University, with a Bachelor of Science degree in General Ministries/Biblical Studies, with a minor in music. He also received a Master of Arts in Practical Theology from SAGU and received his Doctorate of Ministry Degree from West Coast Seminary.

Reverend Barker was ordained by the Assemblies of God in 1989. He began his ministry in the South Texas District in 1984 as youth & music minister and continued his ministry as Pastor, Executive Presbyter (2006 – 2009) and Executive Secretary-Treasurer (2009 – 2011) in the South Texas District, where he served until his election as the South Texas District Superintendent in 2011.

By virtue of his district office, Reverend Barker is a member of the District's Executive Presbytery and the General Presbytery of the General Council of the Assemblies of God, Springfield, Missouri. He is a member of the Executive Board of Regents for Southwestern Assemblies of God University, Waxahachie, Texas, and SAGU-American Indian College, Phoenix, Arizona. He is a member of the Board of Directors of Pleasant Hills Children's Home, Fairfield, Texas, as well as numerous other boards and committees.

Reverend Barker and his wife, Jill, married in 1983, have been blessed with two daughters. Jordin and her husband, Stancle Williams, who serves as the South Texas District Youth Director. Abrielle and her husband, Nolan McLaughlin are church planters of Motion Church in San Antonio. The Barkers have five grandchildren, Braylen, Emory and Landon Williams and Kingston and London McLaughlin.

His unique style of pulpit ministry and musical background challenges the body of Christ, with an appeal that reaches the generations.

A Final Word

You can find Tim on the South Texas District website at www.stxag.org, on Facebook, or at his Houston office when he's not traveling his home state ministering in the churches across the South Texas District.

He'd be thrilled to connect with you and share stories of God's faithfulness.

Study Guide Answers

Includes:

Questions and Answers
from each chapter ...

... *includes page numbers for your convenience.*

Chapter One
Study Guide

1. Authenticity is the mark of a true Christian. What gives us authenticity in the eyes of the world?

   Answer: Our behavior, i.e., the fruit of the Spirit, p. 1

2. Matthew 7:15 speaks of "false prophets." What makes someone a false prophet?

   Answer: Different in appearance and substance; i.e., looks like a sheep but inwardly is like a wolf, p 2

3. In Matthew 7:16-23, we learn how to recognize a true follower of Jesus. Describe the process as illustrated by the Master.

   Answer: Whether they bear good fruit or bad, p 3

4. What will happen to the Christian who cries, "Lord, Lord," but shows no evidence of good fruit?

   Answer: Cast into the fire; i.e., sent away from the presence of Jesus, pp 4-5

5. What is the key ingredient to producing true spiritual fruit in Christ?

   Answer: To be connected to Christ; i.e., remain in Him in an ongoing relationship, pp 6-7

6. What is the difference between "gifts" and the "fruit" of the Spirit?

> Answer: Gifts are the skills we possess, and fruit is the love (or character) we exhibit, pp 8-9

7. Of spiritual gifts and fruit, which is more important and why?

> Answer: Fruit (or character or love). Our gifts are sounding brass and tinkling cymbals (i.e., useless) otherwise, p 9

Chapter Two
Study Guide

1. Joy in the Bible rarely indicates a "peaceful" and "transcendent state." Yet, joy is intricately intertwined with love. How are joy and love connected?

    Answer: Joy is love's strength, p 14

2. God gives us our greatest opportunity for joy during what times?

    Answer: During tribulations, i.e., in the very process of our struggles and painful events, pp 15

3. Paul challenged the Macedonian Churches during one of their most difficult times. What was the challenge and how did it provide an opportunity for joy?

    Answer: Paul asked the financially strapped Macedonians to give money to the believers in Jerusalem. They would learn that material possessions are not our source of joy. Our joy is based in the world to come, pp 16-17

4. Why does Jesus tell us we can be filled with joy even during times of grief?

    Answer: Grief (mourning) is only for a moment. We have a purpose and a future in Christ that supersedes our grief, p 20

5. The story of Paul and Silas reveals the secret to turning our joy into our strength during hard times. What lesson can we learn from their time in prison?

> Answer: They began to sing praises to God in song in the midst of horrible pain, p 22

6. What is the ultimate result of people seeing the joy of Christ in us?

> Answer: The proclamation of the Gospel as lived out through our example, i.e., people get saved, p 24

7. Joy is a fruit of the Spirit. What does it reveal about our relationship with God?

> Answer: God's Spirit is at work in our life, p 24

Chapter Three
Study Guide

1. Why is the world's peace always temporary?

    Answer: It is based on the fear of mutual destruction, p 28

2. How is God's peace different from the world's peace?

    Answer: It is based on the power of love and God's Spirit at work in us, p 28

3. Our peace in God comes through our fellowship with Him. How do we bring this fellowship about?

    Answer: Through faith in Christ, i.e., salvation, p 29

4. What do our emotions have to do with the peace we wish to find in God?

    Answer: We must make a commitment to change the use of our emotions and feelings to do something wholesome instead of something destructive, i.e., offer forgiveness rather than retaliation for the wrongs done to us by others, p 30

5. Mankind's peace is very tenuous. Because it can disappear so quickly, how does that affect us as people?

Answer: We become filled with despair and fear, p 31

6. Describe the difference in God's peace that allows the Christian to "not let our hearts be troubled or afraid."

Answer: God's peace is neither fragile nor fleeting, i.e., it is forever, p 31

7. The city of Jerusalem has never lived up to its name "city of peace." How/when will that be different in the future?

Answer: The New Jerusalem, i.e., Heaven, will be filled with the peace of God forever, in the same way His peace lives in our hearts today, p 35

Chapter Four
Study Guide

1. Why does the Word focus so strongly on patience as an aspect of the fruit of the Spirit?

    Answer: Patience helps to develop stability in our walk with God, p 39

2. We can misunderstand God's patience as being slow concerning His promises. What is God's real reason (from His vantage point) for His enduring patience?

    Answer: God desires that some may come to salvation, i.e., be saved, pp 40-41

3. We can learn a character lesson from God's patience with us. What does God wish us to learn?

    Answer: To be patient with others who are still sinners (as well as those who are saints), p 42

4. Patience is a characteristic of love. How are patience and love connected, and why is patience so important to love?

    Answer: Patience is love's stability, and without it, all stability is gone, p 44

5. What do we mean when we say that Christians are a backwards people?

Answer: The world looks backwards, i.e., to their past, and as Christians, we look to the future. We know what's coming, pp 45-46

6. How do so many Christians miss out on blessings God intends for them?

Answer: Acting too soon, i.e., not being patient with God, p 46

7. Connect the value of patience with developing our Christian character.

Answer: Character needs time and challenges to develop, which requires patience, p 46

Chapter Five
Study Guide

1. God's kindness can mean something vastly different for sinners and saints. Describe the difference between the two.

   Answer: It demonstrates the love and power of God to the sinner, while the saint gets to experience that power and love, p 51

2. Paul lists six ways the saints at Corinth were being unkind to one another. Tell how at least three of these can apply to the modern church.

   Answer: (samples) 1. Factions: prioritizing adults vs. the youth 2. Lawsuits: over failed business ventures 3. Marriage difficulties: inappropriate texting among church members 4. Disrespecting church leaders: gossiping or complaining about the pastor 5. Unkind to each other during communion: refusing to greet people of different financial backgrounds 6. Confusing use of spiritual gifts: praying in tongues when there is no interpretation, pp 52-53

3. Give three steps to improve kindness in ourselves and in the church body. (Think grapes!)

Answer: 1. Growing 2. Crushing 3. Aging until we are mellow with kindness, pp 53-54

4. Describe the difference between the world's concept of kindness and that expected of the saints.

Answer: The world sees kindness as being polite. The saint forgives divinely and treats an enemy well when they don't deserve it, p 54-55

5. Kindness is not an automatic fruit of the Spirit, meaning we don't automatically become kind when we receive the infilling of the Holy Spirit. What else does kindness require?

Answer: Our efforts (combined with the Spirit), p 57

6. The goal of politeness is to make people feel good. Describe the goal of kindness (which can't be faked).

Answer: To reveal God's love to others, p 58

7. What is the personal benefit we derive from showing the kindness of Christ to those around us?

Answer: It makes us strong, not weak, p 59

Chapter Six
Study Guide

1. What is our reason for doing good once we are infilled with the Spirit?

    Answer: It is now in our spiritual nature to do so, p 64

2. During the story of Creation, God repeatedly says, "It is good." Explain why.

    Answer: Creation now bore the stamp of His divine character, that of innate goodness, p 66

3. Why will unbelievers be sorely disappointed even though they think they have lived a "good" life?

    Answer: No one is saved by his or her own good works, i.e., mankind's goodness is false and will not suffice for entrance into heaven, pp 66

4. Why can unbelievers not achieve heaven through their own "goodness" or works?

    Answer: True goodness is not natural but divine or spiritual, pp 67

5. Why was the rich young man so disappointed in Jesus' answer to the question, "What must I do to have eternal life?"

    Answer: He wanted to do "one good thing" not

live a righteous life to enter heaven, p 69

6. What is vital for us to do before we ask Jesus the question, "What must I do …"?

Answer: First, we must have a relationship with God, p 71

7. The essence of goodness involves more than kindness, politeness, or good manners. In fact, it doesn't focus on us at all. What is the true essence of goodness?

Answer: Seeking God for others, i.e., development of our character in order to benefit others, p 74

Chapter Seven
Study Guide

1. Our modern culture values success over many other things, yet Jesus never taught on success. What did the Master prioritize instead and how do we know?

    Answer: Faithfulness. He says, "Well done, you faithful servant." p 77

2. Hosea saw the faithlessness rampant in Israel. How did the prophet attempt to redirect the nation back onto the righteous path that God required?

    Answer: He demonstrated faithfulness, i.e., remained faithful to his immoral wife, as well as called for it from the people, p 80

3. What result did Israel's faithlessness have besides the moral and spiritual degradation of the nation?

    Answer: Environmental collapse as revealed in Hosea 4:3, p 81-82

4. As Israel continued to chase success and prosperity rather than faithfulness to God, what happened in their lives?

    Answer: The emptier their lives became, p 84

5. What happens to a people when God's call to return to faithfulness is ignored on an ongoing basis?

Answer: Destruction. Israel never listened to Hosea, and the Northern Kingdom (Israel) was destroyed and never recovered, p 84-85

6. How important is it to "choose" faithfulness when we are infilled with the Holy Spirit?

Answer: It's not a choice. It's standard equipment for the Spirit-filled believer, p 86

7. Our faithfulness to God can be related to the U.S. Marine's signature motto. What is it and what does it mean?

Answer: SEMPER FI which means, "Always Faithful," p 87

Chapter Eight
Study Guide

1. Gentleness in the Bible means something other than soft-spoken or easily intimidated. Where did this term for "strength under control" originate?

   Answer: From a term for a wild horse trained to a bit and bridle, p 91

2. What aspect of "LOVE" does "GENTLENESS" reveal?

   Answer: Humility, which is God-controlled (not self-controlled), p 92

3. Jesus asks us to "take His yoke upon us." Describe an easy way to picture what He means.

   Answer: We are paired like a new ox with a seasoned one, where our companion leads and does most of the work, p 92-93

4. What is the companion aspect of the attribute of gentleness? (Hint, think of Moses.)

   Answer: Humility, i.e., developing strength by following Jesus, p 94

5. Why does living for Christ make so many people in the world uncomfortable?

   Answer: It means yielding up control of one's life,

and our culture sees this as a weakness, p 94

6. Does being used by God give us the right to speak ill of those we disapprove of? Explain your answer.

> Answer: No. Aaron and Miriam spoke against Moses, God's favored one, and God called them out for it, p 97

7. Give another word for gentleness and where we find it in the Bible.

> Answer: Meekness. The Greek word for gentleness is translated as meek in the Beatitudes, p 99-100

Chapter Nine
Study Guide

1. Why is it so important to learn self-control in our Christian walk?

   Answer: Failure to conquer ourselves leaves us unproductive, unfilled, and sometimes broken and depressed, p 103

2. Self-control not only affects us, but it also affects others, too. Who is most affected if we fail to exhibit self-control?

   Answer: The next generation of undisciplined lives, p 104

3. The Universe seems peaceful and orderly, with planets and even galaxies right where we expect them to be. How do we know this "peacefulness" is not the case?

   Answer. Paul describes the Universe as "groaning" because of sin, p 106

4. Salvation is given to us without cost, and we are saved by grace. Yet, to maintain a committed life in Christ, what else is necessary?

   Answer: Self-control. The Holy Spirit is our helper in this area, pp 107

5. Paul compares salvation to a race. What must all contestants do to come in first place?

> Answer: Exercise self-control, i.e., train (or run in a way to get the prize), p 109

6. How did Paul see himself differently as a leader in the early Church?

> Answer: He carried more responsibility to show self-control or he might lose the prize himself, p 110

7. Of the eight characteristics of the fruit of the Spirit, only one (self-control) is directed back at us. Why is this concept so vital in our Christian walk?

> Answer: No progress in a believer's life can occur without self-control, for self-control is love's victory, p 113

Additional Books by Tim R. Barker

If you liked this book, you may be interested in additional books Tim has written. Turn the page for short descriptions of each book. All are available on Amazon.

This soul-building, introspective 4-book series reveals Tim's innermost heart on subjects that affect all of us, from Cooperation to Loyalty to The Truth of Salvation and more.

The books in this series include:

My Jesus Journey
My Jesus Journey: Crescendo
My Jesus Journey: Glissando
My Jesus Journey: Rhapsody

In this book, you will read of God's favor and His redemption, for you are chosen and forgiven. In Jesus, you can find the rest you desire, for at His feet, His joy becomes whole.

Come to Jesus today. He holds His hand out to you.

The Lord with Us
from the Book of Hebrews

Do you have a relationship with Jesus? The rewards are great, but if we fail to heed the warnings in the Word, the consequences are also great.

Even if we call ourselves Christian, we must live according to God's will. The Lord is with us when we walk with Him. This is the message from the book of Hebrews.

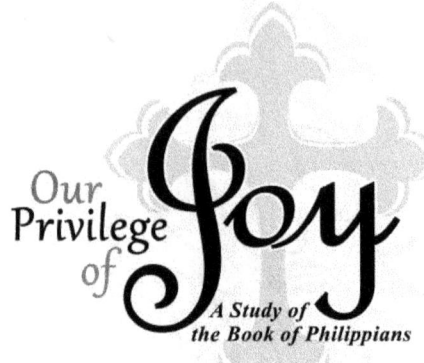

Our Privilege of Joy
A Study of the Book of Philippians

Philippians is our blueprint from the Father, our plan for joy. It was written by the hand of Paul during his time in a Roman prison, but the voice is the Father's, entreating us to lift our hands in praise to Him, and to find joy even in the difficult parts of our lives.

NAMES OF GOD

Our name tells people who we are.

What about the name Christian? That's what the followers of Jesus call themselves. What information can people glean about us when we put a fish symbol on the bumper of our car, or we wear a cross around our neck? And, importantly, do our actions live up to their expectations?

This book is an in-depth teaching about the ten names of God.

The Vision of Nehemiah
God's Plan for Righteous Living

The Book of Nehemiah reveals a vital truth that our instant society often overlooks. Determination can take us only so far in achieving the goals God has for today's Church.

Winning the lost for Christ takes preparation in both our time and our finances. We become the "right stuff" for achieving God's plan when we are willing to risk everything for Him.

God's Revelation and Your Future

The book of Revelation is first and foremost a revelation about Jesus, not just the future.

John reveals Christ as the King of Glory, the conqueror, the one in charge of history, the one who alone controls the future, controls the nations, controls all the universe! This is the Jesus who is coming!

The book of Revelation shows us the glorified Christ and the certainty of His ruling over all things. We are not stumbling toward an uncertain future, but we must be in fellowship with the King!

Truth, Love & Redemption

The Holy Spirit For Today

There is no greater empowerment for the Christian of today than to seek out the Holy Spirit. It was considered vital in the early days of Christendom. Now, many times it is pushed aside as "for then" and not "for now."

We are in greater need of the truth, love, and redemption that flows from an encounter with the Holy Spirit than ever before. The Scriptures tell us that our realization of our need for Christ flows from the Spirit. Even before we accept Christ, the Holy Spirit draws us to Him.

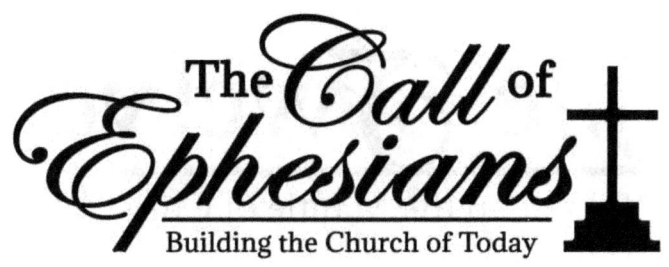

Paul understood that legalism can become a hindrance to our Christian walk and that we must focus on Christ and Christ alone. When our faith hits the road, God is there with us. He challenges us to trust Him to walk at our side through every challenge we might face.

When we do, we become mighty warriors in God's army.

That's Paul's message in a nutshell, and it's vital we take it to heart.

The Twelve
Taking up the Mantle of Christ

Twelve men were chosen to fulfill Christ's legacy on the earth.

Eleven looked to Jesus for the answers to life's questions. One chose the world and the world failed him.

These men were as varied as the members of our modern church, at times at odds with one another, but forged by Jesus into a single unit that overcame everything the devil could throw at them. What lesson can we learn from them?

Our only option is to choose Christ.

End Times

Scripture provides us a timeline of events that signal that the end is coming soon.
1. The Church Age
2. The Rapture of the Church
3. The Tribulation
4. The Second Coming of Jesus Christ
5. The Millennium
6. The Great White Throne Judgment
7. New Heavens and New Earth

Follow along through each of these Biblical timeline events.

Anticipating the Return of Christ

Are we waiting or are we watching for His appearance in the skies? The difference is in being ready for His return and risking missing Him altogether.

This book covers six areas of preparation for the Return of Christ.

1. Waiting
2. Mindful
3. Joyful
4. Praying
5. Thanking
6. Faithful.

Are you anticipating Christ's return? I am.

Your Invitation to Christ

Your Invitation to Christ guarantees six things. Once you accept Christ's invitation you can:

1. Rest. It's yours in the midst of whatever comes your way.
2. See. Your eyes are opened to the supernatural.
3. Follow. Christ is your only true leader.
4. Drink. The ambrosia of Jesus becomes yours.
5. Dine. You will find renewal in your fellowship with your Lord.
6. Inherit. The Kingdom will one day be yours. It's called Heaven.

Salvation comes through Christ. God desires our presence, and we draw closer to Him through our Lord and Savior, Jesus.

www.ingramcontent.com/pod-product-compliance
Lightning Source LLC
Chambersburg PA
CBHW051837090426
42736CB00011B/1853